"*Preaching Politics* is a compelling narrative that astutely examines the nexus between religion and politics, and the modern dilemmas faced today by the Christian church and people of faith. Clay Stauffer is a friend and Tennessee native who artfully draws from his own personal experiences to inform how our lives can continue to benefit and grow from the Gospel of Jesus Christ."
 — Former U.S. Senate Majority Leader William H. Frist, M.D., (R)

"Clay is a good man and a great preacher. He wrestles with the same issues as his large congregation, and helps them understand each other and, more importantly, Jesus. *Preaching Politics* gives everyone helpful advice for coping with many of the problems of today's world. Clay is married to a physician, but he, too, is a healer."
 — U.S. Representative Jim Cooper (D)

"Clay Stauffer is not afraid to take on the tough issues! Thankfully, he approaches these issues with a spirit of grace and a willingness to listen. The New Testament encourages us to 'speak the truth with love.' Clay's new book attempts to do just that."
 — Governor Bill Haslam (R)

"Clay Stauffer's amazing book does two things to this wealthy septuagenarian: It brings me to my knees in prayer and challenges me to open my wallet and my life for spiritual warfare to a dying world."
 — Cal Turner, Jr., former Chairman and CEO, Dollar General

"Clay Stauffer brings a welcome voice of moderation to charged debates in American religion and politics. In the role of preacher to a widely diverse community, he urges us to let Jesus' words be the point of reference. Seeking a place of unity, he nevertheless dares to wade into one of the trickiest areas of all—money and possessions—and gives us all something to think about."

— Sharon Watkins, General Minister and President of the Christian Church (Disciples of Christ) and Author of *Whole: A Call to Unity in Our Fragmented World*

"Preaching when done with reverence and authenticity is a sweet and brutal dance. When one dares wrestle with the issues of the day the dance is guaranteed to throw the preacher and/or congregant off balance. Clay Stauffer's publication offers the reader a methodology of sacred balance to navigate the undercurrents of political ideas and prophetic witness. As a professor and pastor I hear the cries of students who desire to engage the world, but are afraid because of an insular tradition or general lack of exposure. This book provides a powerful witness and needed contribution to a discipline of study desperate for prophetic voices."

— Otis Moss III, Senior Pastor, Trinity United Church of Christ, Chicago

"The preaching task may be harder than it has ever been, and the temptation to make the task easier by avoiding topics listeners find uncomfortable is very much with us. It is this temptation Clay Stauffer faces in his important book. Preachers will see themselves and their churches on every page, and will find Stauffer an excellent conversation partner as they too face the 'preaching dilemma' together."

— William Brosend, The School of Theology, Sewanee, and Author of *The Preaching of Jesus* and *James and Jude*

"Clay Stauffer is a pastor who knows what it's like firsthand to struggle with contemporary American sins, particularly the sin of our materialism. Like any good pastor Clay tries to listen to his congregation, listening also to some of the leading Christian thinkers. As he listens, he attempts to hear commonalities, opportunities for confluence of seemingly competing opinions, and in all things to build up the church as the Body of Christ with a responsibility to witness to God's beloved but rebellious world. I learned from Clay's book and commend it to churches struggling with fidelity to Christ in our American context."

    — Will Willimon, Professor of the Practice of Christian Ministry, Duke Divinity School, and United Methodist Bishop, retired

"Stauffer provides a helpful guide for understanding the need and biblical justification for preaching about the politically contentious issues of money, greed, and power within a capitalist society. With sound exegesis of key teachings of Jesus on money and faith, as well as robust theological engagement with Stanley Hauerwas and Adam Hamilton, this book is useful for both preaching and leading Bible studies. Stauffer encourages, equips and emboldens preachers to tackle these issues from the study and the pulpit with renewed confidence."

    — Leah D. Schade, Author of *Creation-Crisis Preaching: Ecology, Theology, and the Pulpit*

"Clay Stauffer takes a thoughtful approach to dealing with difficult political issues facing the church in an increasingly polarized and materialistic society. From his pulpit in a politically diverse and affluent congregation, Clay deals with these issues firsthand. While this book will be a guide for pastors, it is just as relevant for those of us who sit in the pews."

    — William F. Carpenter III, Chairman and CEO, LifePoint Health.

"It is a mistake to think Jesus was not political. He led a movement of reform, preaching about the problems of empire, casting a vision of a healed and whole society in which those on the margins are seen and heard as leaders— one in which the hungry are fed, the destitute redeemed, and the strangers welcomed. The gospel is radical political business. Here is a book for our time, a time in which prophetic preaching must capture the imaginations and hearts of those in the pew to live God's dream. Clay Stauffer uses the teachings of Jesus, and the work of Methodist pastor Adam Hamilton and Duke ethicist Stanley Hauerwas to encourage preaching for the polis—for the people—as he provides help for the visionary preacher in all of us."

— Jacqui Lewis, Senior Minister, Middle Collegiate Church, and host, *Just Faith* at ShiftMSNBC

PREACHING
POLITICS

To my loving wife, Megan, and my children, Montgomery and Clayton, who are growing up in a constantly changing world that finds itself more and more polarized. As Karl Barth said, "May you approach each day with a Bible in one hand and a newspaper in the other."

PREACHING POLITICS

Proclaiming Jesus
in an Age of Money,
Power, and Partisanship

CLAY STAUFFER

CHALICE
PRESS
ST. LOUIS, MISSOURI

Cover design: Jesse Turri

www.chalicepress.com

Print: 9780827231344

EPUB: 9780827231351   EPDF: 9780827231368

Library of Congress Cataloging-in-Publication Data

Names: Stauffer, Clay, 1980- author.
Title: Preaching politics : proclaiming Jesus in an age of money,
    power, and partisanship / by Clay Stauffer.
Description: First [edition]. | St. Louis : Chalice Press, 2016. |
    Includes bibliographical references and index. | Description based
    on print version record and CIP data provided by publisher;
    resource not viewed.
Identifiers: LCCN 2015048596 (print) | LCCN 2015043537 (ebook) |
    ISBN 9780827231351 (epub) | ISBN 9780827231368 (epdf) |
    ISBN 9780827231344 (pbk. : alk. paper)
Subjects: LCSH: Preaching. | Christianity and politics.
Classification: LCC BV4235.P7 (print) | LCC BV4235.P7 S73 2016
    (ebook) | DDC 251—dc23
LC record available at http://lccn.loc.gov/2015048596

Printed in the United States of America

Contents

Refusing to Play It Safe

Shortly before this book went to press, I sat down at a coffee shop close to my church with a seasoned politician whom I respect despite the fact that we don't always see eye to eye on every issue. He is older than I am and has seen more than his share of stump speeches, sermons, elections, political pandering, and partisan games. He also seems to respect me regardless of my relative youth and our differences on politics, faith, social policy, and the like. But we each share a love of this great nation, our home state of Tennessee, and the city of Nashville. And we each love our coffee, prepared differently, of course. On this occasion we had another civil conversation—one that included the purpose and intent of this book.

"Clay, I don't know why you would want to write a book about preaching politics," he said. "I've always considered what you do to be above the political fray, a much more noble profession than mine. Why would you want to dive into the swamp? It doesn't seem necessary. I just don't want you to regret this later in your life."

His observation caught me off guard at 6:45 in the morning. I was still waking up. And to be honest, what he said rattled me. Why *do* I want to talk about the potential pitfalls of preaching politics? Why do I want to "dirty myself" in the realm of politicians who have low-digit approval ratings? Why would I want to open Pandora's Box and unleash the howls of those who say politics has no place in the pulpit? Shouldn't ministers of the gospel play it safe and stay as far away from politics as possible? Aren't millennials staying away from the church because they believe it is too political? Haven't preachers on both ends of the spectrum managed to offend enough people and do enough damage already?

My response to these questions has its roots in the denominational ethos that I grew up in and in which I now minister. At thirty-five years of age, I am in my ninth year as senior minister of Woodmont Christian Church (Disciples of Christ). I am also a fourth-generation pastor, following my father, grandfather, and great-grandfather. In the Stone-Campbell tradition that gave birth to my denomination, we say that we "agree to disagree" when it comes to controversial issues that tend to divide Christians. We stress the unity of Christ's church and seek to maintain it. "In essentials, unity; in nonessentials, liberty; but in all things love." That's our mantra. This is what we strive to live out in our local churches.

And yet, throughout my adult life, I have watched the church argue, fight, and, in many cases, tear itself apart over a variety of issues. How many issues are there in American society that can be debated eternally without either side conceding an inch of moral high ground? As we prepare for another heated presidential race (2016), many theologians and preachers will endorse a variety of candidates and stake their partisan positions. Controversial issues tend to make their way from the public square and into the pews. Same-sex marriage is just one of many recent examples. This topic has recently dominated the discussion in many congregations and denominations, and among ministers, families, and friends. It has overshadowed many other important topics—many of which, in my view at least, matter far more than this issue does. When the U.S. Supreme Court granted civil-rights status to same-sex unions and ruled that those unions are marriages, I immediately thought less about my own perspective and more about what the Court's decision would mean for the future of Christianity and the church. My fear was that an ongoing polarization within Christianity would widen, leaving us with conservative churches, liberal churches, and not much in between. Disagreements, passions, and emotions abound. I see this as a growing problem that must be identified and addressed. Christian tribalism has always been the easy way out. Living and preaching in the tension are admirable but never easy. Civil dialogue and mutual respect are absolutely necessary if a united church is to have a future.

Many people already claim that we live in a post-Christian world where the church has lost its influence in society. Some of them point to this Supreme Court ruling on marriage as clear evidence that the church has failed to be a moral light. Others, however, say the Court's ruling will now give the church a chance to reach people it has alienated and marginalized from the pews for years. Who is right? Each side uses scripture to defend its position. The church's unity is taking another major hit. In fact, the ugliness and raw emotion of the debate itself (regardless of which side people are on) seem to bring out the worst in people and have driven many good people away from the church.

The book you hold in your hands is not about this issue or any other single political issue but rather about *how* we debate *any* political issue, and the potential divisions and stressors that pastors and preachers face on a regular basis . Our congregations are split along political, social, and moral lines. Often the moral is wrapped up in the political, and the politics lead to certain perceptions of one another's theological and biblical beliefs. Some people and churches feel that their version of Christianity is superior. Furthermore, obvious divisions related to socioeconomic class and lifestyle differences are also a reality for many churches. Growing materialism, the glorification of money, rampant consumerism, the constant quest for more, and a false sense of security present real challenges to our spiritual lives and the church of the future. As I will contend, Jesus still speaks to all these things.

I intend to probe this confusing and often damaging mix of beliefs, opinions, and inferences within the Christian faith. I will do this using Luke's portrait of Jesus and some of his teachings, as well as by drawing on the fine work of distinguished scholars. What we find as we go along may be surprising, and it will certainly be challenging—regardless of your political or theological persuasion.

My hope is that this book will help us foster a more productive approach to ministry, preaching, and community in our generation and beyond—an approach that will permit differences that refuse to yield to division; an approach that will produce constructive dialogue instead of diatribes, promote the faith's essentials over its nonessentials, and make Christianity more attractive to a world still very much in need of the gospel of Jesus Christ.

Clay Stauffer
Nashville, Tennessee
Christmas 2015

CHAPTER 1

* * * * * * * * * * * * * *

Preachers, Politics, and Partisanship

Every Sunday preachers across the United States enter their pulpits attempting to deliver faithfully sermons that convey the truth of God's word in ways that speak pastorally and prophetically to the lives of those in their congregations. Any minister charged with this weekly task is keenly aware of this ongoing challenge—requiring courage, creativity, study, exegesis, preparation, revision, and delivery. What makes the preaching task difficult is that many congregations are composed of members with diverse backgrounds and political ideologies. On any given Sunday morning at Woodmont Christian Church in Nashville, I look out and see liberals and conservatives, Democrats and Republicans, super wealthy CEOs and members of the working class sitting on the same pew, all expecting to hear a word from God. What unites them is a common belief in Christ. What often separates them are political tendencies and socioeconomic realities.

In our tradition, the Christian Church (Disciples of Christ), we take great pride in this diversity. Christian unity is our polar star. We agree to disagree. Our denomination's slogan says that we are a "movement for wholeness in a fragmented world."[1] We honor Alexander Campbell's and Barton Stone's vision to unite all Christians regardless of their differences. Yet I will be the first to admit that, as good as this sounds, it is not an easy task for the one charged with delivering the sermon.

Many in the pews feel that preaching and politics should never be intertwined, especially if you happen to proclaim a position or perspective with which they disagree. Some of this stems from the old adage that faith and politics are two subjects that should not be discussed or debated in polite company, at a dinner party, in casual conversation, in a social situation, or—at least when it comes to politics—in the pulpit. Why? Because these two topics incite an emotional and even visceral response from so many people. Most people in our world maintain strong opinions and viewpoints on these topics, and they have formed their views over time through thought, reflection, and experience. Other opinions have been systematically (and often thoughtlessly) passed down from family members, friends, churches, and communities.

In my view, the emotion and passion that arise when faith and politics meet illustrate why these topics *should* be discussed. There is a correlation between the two. We cannot deny that faith is often linked to politics, and many political candidates use the language and rhetoric of faith to excite and motivate their supporters. In a similar manner, certain preachers are also guilty of using political rhetoric to subvert a text, motivate a base, and gain a following. Context always matters when it comes to preaching.

The United States is a country with a unique religious history. Former *Newsweek* editor Jon Meacham makes this case in his 2006 book *American Gospel: God, the Founding Fathers, and the Making of a Nation*: "The great goodness about America—the American Gospel, if you will—is that religion shapes the life of the nation without strangling it. Belief in God is central to the country's experience, yet for the broad center, faith is a matter of choice, not coercion, and the legacy of the Founding Fathers is that the sensible center holds."[2] Meacham clearly indicates that the Founding Fathers sought to establish a nation where religious freedom was pivotal and could not be taken away by the government or any human being. The *Declaration of Independence* states that "all men are created equal, that they are endowed by their Creator with certain inalienable Rights."[3] Thomas Jefferson and the other Founders struggled to find the proper place for religion in

American life. One could make the case that their endeavor proved successful. The Founders' intention was to create a Republic that maintained a separation of church and state, but in no way did that mean a complete separation of faith and politics. These two concepts are fundamentally different, and many individuals and groups fail to recognize and appreciate the distinction. This misunderstanding has led to what has been called an estranged relationship between faith and politics. The relationship is there, but preachers often struggle with how to find a balance between them in homiletics.

Many preachers experience this tension on a regular basis, especially if serving a politically diverse congregation. Jesus spoke truth to power in his day and calls us to courageously do the same. Churches are tax-exempt as 501C3 organizations. By law a church (or other religious organization) cannot officially endorse political candidates or parties without putting that tax-exempt status in jeopardy. However, this does not mean that churches and preachers must avoid controversial topics. Faithfully preaching the gospel of Jesus Christ requires taking bold and prophetic stands when it comes to particular issues and situations. There is a political side to Jesus' life and ministry that cannot be ignored. The dilemma for many preachers is that taking "prophetic" stands that are anti-war, anti-poverty, and that promote social inclusion often lead to a minister being labeled as "liberal." But are such stands liberal, or are they simply biblical? If we take the time to seriously study and reflect upon the life and ministry of Jesus of Nazareth as recorded in the gospels—including what he did, what he said, and how he treated others—should our findings influence our politics? I would argue yes. Still, some will say that Jesus was apolitical. I grant that he may not have been political in the way we define that word today (Red, Blue, etc.), but he was certainly a political figure who proclaimed a Kingdom that is very different from the kingdoms of this world.

Toward the end of his book *Disruptive Grace,* Old Testament scholar and prophetic theologian Walter Brueggemann makes the case that preaching will be very challenging yet absolutely necessary in the coming century. He even refers to the preaching task resulting from healthy biblical exegesis as "urgent." He gives the following reasons:

- The matter is urgent because our consumer economy reduces everything and everyone to a commodity, just as Pharaoh had done.

- The matter is urgent because U.S. militarism now stalks the earth and generates resistance among local cultures and local economies; the enormous, unrestrained power of the U.S. military is itself a reflection of the pervasive violence that marks our society.

- The matter is urgent because the public infrastructure of our society—health, education, housing, jobs—all is at risk, and we increasingly seek to go "on the cheap" about everything except military assertiveness.

- The matter is urgent because our use and abuse of the earth is rapacious and cannot be sustained, even in the interest of a growing economy.[4]

Brueggemann views the God we find in both the Old and New Testaments as calling us not to remain silent but to speak out boldly in the face of these issues. However, bold preaching is not always well received, especially in affluent contexts. To use two examples, a discussion of the U.S. military's role around the world or the pros and cons of our welfare system will evoke profound disagreements among well-meaning Christians.

Partisan Divisions within Congregations

In 2012, Mike Slaughter, Charles Gutenson, and Robert Jones published a fascinating book titled *Hijacked: Responding to the Partisan Church Divide*. It is well-written, well-researched, and most helpful in understanding what has caused the partisan divide in churches and how to deal with political tension and disagreement within a congregation. The authors frame the question well: "Why is it, then, that we have allowed political partisanship to enter so deeply into our churches? And, perhaps more importantly, how is it that we have allowed those differences to divide us, to create obstacles among us, and to have created an environment in which one or the other can be somehow considered less a 'follower of Jesus' simply on the basis of one being the supporter of a particular party or ideology?"[5] They argue that many people in our society believe that if you are a Christian, you will identify with a particular party and hold deep convictions on certain issues. Everything is black and white, and there is no grey. Of course, life is not that simple, but it is amazing how many people feel this way when it comes to politics and controversial issues. Slaughter and Gutenson believe that it is problematic when Christians combine theology with a certain brand of politics and try to categorize everybody as either "liberal" or "conservative." "It seems popular lore in contemporary American culture to assume that there are only two theopolitical positions. According to the popular way of categorizing people, there are conservatives and liberals. If you are conservative, then you are politically and theologically conservative; if you are liberal, then you are politically and theologically liberal."[6]

The words *liberal* and *conservative* are loaded terms in our culture. And there is little consensus as to what they mean. "One can be theologically conservative and politically conservative; one can be theologically liberal and politically conservative; one can be theologically conservative and politically liberal; and one can be theologically liberal and politically liberal."[7] Simply throwing around the terms "liberal" and "conservative" is not very helpful. It is actually part of the problem.

In his book *The Happiness Hypothesis,* social psychologist Jonathan Haidt shows that both liberals and conservatives make valuable contributions to society because of their different interests and passions.

> My research confirms the common perception that liberals are experts in thinking about issues of victimization, equality, autonomy, and the rights of individuals, particularly those of minorities and non-conformists. Conservatives, on the other hand, are experts in thinking about loyalty to the group, respect for authority and tradition, and sacredness. When one side overwhelms the other, the results are likely to be ugly. A society without liberals would be harsh and oppressive to many individuals. A society without

conservatives would lose many of the social structures and constraints that Durkeim showed are so valuable.[8]

This is also the case in the case in the church, demonstrating the ongoing need for mutual respect and healthy dialogue.

Slaughter and Gutenson address the fact that many Christians say they are willing to "agree to disagree" when it comes to political issues, but in reality many are unable to actually do this.

> Let's face it, we as Christians are perhaps as unsuccessful as any at being able to disagree passionately, while still maintaining fellowship with those with whom we disagree. As Christians, it is true that we need to look for unity in the things essential to the faith. It is true that we need to allow diversity of opinion on things that are not essential. But regardless of whether we agree or disagree, it is a fact that we are to always model love for one another.[9]

What should identify and distinguish Christians is the abiding love and respect that we have for each another. This gets tested when we find ourselves at odds with other church members. The way disagreements are handled, especially within the church, is a direct reflection of spiritual depth and maturity: "Remember that Jesus said Christians would be known, not by their ability to draw lines between themselves and those with whom they disagree, not by their ability to hold only true opinions on all matters, but rather by their love for one another quite apart from whether they fully agree on all the issues."[10]

We now live in a culture in which tolerance, healthy dialogue, and mutual respect seem to be in short supply. A primary reason for this is the "sound-bite" culture driven by twenty-four-hour cable news that thrives on pitting extreme positions against each other. The most hostile, partisan, and extreme politicians and faith leaders get the media coverage and air time. The reason? They are not afraid of conflict and confrontation. News has turned into arguing, yelling, pandering, and entertainment. Anybody willing to compromise, find middle ground, and work with leaders of another party is viewed as "selling out." Unfortunately, the same is often true when it comes to religious leaders and pastors. Those who hold the extreme positions and stir the greatest controversy get the airtime.

However, there is something to be said about being passionate when it comes to faith and core beliefs. In the church, when two passionate, well-educated people are at odds with each other, pride and ego create division. I serve an affluent, well-educated church in Nashville. The leaders and members of our church all have strong opinions. As a pastor and preacher, my role is to encourage them to maintain that passion while not using it as a way of lashing out or denigrating somebody else. Passion is good, but only if it is channeled in the right way. In the church, it is often true that the more deeply convicted people are about an issue, the more passionate they are and the less willing they are to listen to other perspectives. So, when it comes to political topics discussed within the church, passions run high.

Slaughter and Gutenson believe that the church must set the example for love, mutual respect, and dialogue. If the church, which is grounded in the love, peace, and tolerance of Jesus Christ, is not able to accomplish this, then we risk allowing partisan differences to divide the beloved community. Again, the preacher and pastor must be the one who leads the effort and encourages others to do the same:

> Members of Christ's Body have been guilty of demeaning and demonizing those with whom they disagree. We have allowed worldly political ideologies to become determining factors for our theology rather than grounding ourselves in a sound biblical theology for determining our politics. Some well-meaning believers have become more passionate about engaging in the heat of partisan political debate than they have been in sharing the good news about Jesus.[11]

Our responsibility is to be Christians first, and Republicans or Democrats second. When these get reversed, the dialogue turns into resentment. In their book, at the end of chapter 6, "The Role of the Local Church," Slaughter and Gutenson sum up what they have been saying: "Unity in Christ will not mean an end to differences. The Democrats and Republicans in our pews will still disagree over the issues and people governing our nation. But if our common mission as disciples takes precedence over our partisan political views, we can live and work for good peaceably together in Jesus' name."[12] When Christians allow partisan and ideological differences to divide the body of Christ, we have missed the goal of forming a community built on love and mutual respect.

Harvard professor Robert Putnam and Notre Dame professor David Campbell published a book in 2010 entitled *American Grace: How Religion Divides and Unites Us.* They deal with partisan politics within congregations. Contrary to what many believe, "[T]he people who are most likely to report political activity at church are liberals who attend a politically homogenous congregation." This may come as a surprise to many who feel as though it is always the Religious Right who use churches and pastors to motivate the base. Putnam and Campbell say, "A longer historical view, however, reminds us that many denominations have long been catalysts for political action on socially progressive, left-leaning causes. Surveys of religious leaders have found that, even today, liberal clergy bring more politics to their churches than do conservative pastors."[13] In light of this, a logical question to ask is: How does a congregation become politically homogenous?

I once served on the staff of a politically homogenous church, The Riverside Church in New York City. In hindsight, I'm not sure how healthy that context really was. Anybody who does not agree with the politics preached there (liberal, Democratic politics) is made to feel very uncomfortable and out of place. Riverside serves as a liberal example of what happens when a church becomes politically homogenous and overtly political. There is no balanced dialogue regarding political issues because, generally speaking, everybody is in the same camp. This would also prove true in a politically conservative congregation such as Thomas Road Baptist Church at Liberty University.

If we take a long look at the history of our nation, it is true that religion has been and continues to be used as a source of inspiration for both the political left and the political right. Both liberals and conservatives get their motivation from the Bible and from their faith. Putnam and Campbell put it this way:

> American history teaches us that religion is neither exclusively left nor right, progressive nor conservative. Instead, religion of different sorts has been associated with political causes of different sorts. On some issues, notably those related to race, religion has been invoked to justify both sides of the debate. In the nineteenth century, religion animated advocates of both abolition and slavery. No one made the point better than Abraham Lincoln, who, in his second inaugural address, referred to the two sides of the Civil War by noting that "both read the same Bible and pray to the same God, and each invokes his aid against the other."[14]

In many ways, this continues to be true. A careful analysis of scripture and even the words of Jesus himself do not lead us all to the same conclusions. So, if there are good people who continue to read the same Bible and come up with different conclusions, that only points to the importance of dialogue. In politically homogenous congregations, there doesn't seem to be much dialogue; mostly we find a lot of what could be called "preaching to the choir."

Statistics show that church attendance and religious affiliation among the younger generations (the Millennials) are in sharp decline. There could be many reasons for this, but Putnam and Campbell argue that over-politicization in churches has been a turnoff to the millennial generation. "The politicization of religion has triggered a negative reaction among some, mostly young, Americans. They have pulled away from religion precisely because they perceive it as an extension of partisan politics with which they do not agree. They see religion tied up with conservative politics, and their aversion to the latter has led them to reject the former."[15] The truth is, both blatantly conservative and liberal politics can drive somebody away from the church. If the message that comes from the pulpit is overtly political, that can and probably will be negatively received even if the person happens to agree with what is said. Preachers must always be careful with the wording they choose.

Phrases such as, "I know this is a divisive issue, but...," and, "I wrestle with this subject myself but feel led to say something about it...," are always wise in presenting potentially divisive topics. There is a prophetic element to Christ's message that cannot be overlooked, and to completely avoid all political topics would mean watering down much of what Jesus had to say. At the same time, how these matters are presented is what matters. Beating a congregation over the head with one point of view usually backfires.

Politics, Money, and Self-Interest

Often times, political differences are directly tied to two subjects: money and self-interest. These topics and their relationship to the spiritual life will be the primary area of focus for this book. In his 2010 book *Rediscovering Values on Wall Street, Main Street, and Your Street,* Jim Wallis wrote in the immediate aftermath of the Great Recession. He talks about the role that greed and instant gratification played in sending our economy off a financial cliff. He says, "Without a clear sense of self, a strong identity, and a community of purpose, it seems our default mode is to identify ourselves by the things we own. We try to convince ourselves and signal to others who we are almost solely by the clothes we wear, the cars we drive, the restaurants we eat at, and the houses we own."[16] When we build our identities and define ourselves by these things, we are setting ourselves up for great disappointment. These are the "treasures on earth" that Jesus warns against. They do not last because they are temporary. Wallis also talks about how materialism has gradually turned our culture into a narcissistic one. The focus is now on "me, me, me." Advancements in technology (iPhones, iPads, social media) have largely contributed to a rise in both individualism and narcissism. "Technology has allowed for the creation and sharing of new information at levels never seen before in human history. But, it has also created an unprecedented number of ways to say 'Look at me'!"[17] Narcissism, greed, and selfishness were significant factors leading to the financial collapse.

In his chapter titled "Enough Is Enough," Wallis talks about the importance of the way that we see our possessions in life:

Is it wrong to have a nice house? No. But do we use that house to be more hospitable? Is it wrong to eat good food? No. But does that food help us become more generous? Is it wrong to have clothes? A television? A computer? No. No. No. But are we becoming more aware of the world around us and more compassionate towards it? With everything we buy, we need to ask ourselves not only if we need it, but what type of person we are becoming when we buy it.[18]

Wallis is clear that there are many lessons to be learned from the financial crisis of 2008–2009. These lessons include not turning the market into God, not becoming greedy, identifying the difference between wants and needs, and looking out for those who have little or nothing. The years following this crisis have been the most difficult since the Great Depression. The recovery has been slow, and time will tell if we have learned anything or not. Wallis says, "Seeing, feeling, and knowing people in difficult straits is what creates empathy. When enough is never enough and greed is good, our lives are in constant tension. There are always more toys to buy, more stuff to accumulate, and much more to worry about. The more we accumulate, the greater our fear and concern that it might all be lost."[19] The key in life is to be satisfied with what we have and not always want more. We should not continually compare ourselves with those who have more because that's a moving target: there will always be others who have more. As Paul eloquently writes in the final chapter of his letter to the Philippians, "I have learned to be content with whatever I have. I know what it is to have little, and I know what it is to have plenty."[20] For Wallis, Paul, and Jesus, the antidotes to narcissism and individualism are the biblical principles of humility and community.

Jonathan Haidt has done extensive research on happiness, meaning, and its relationship to consumerism and materialism. In *The Happiness Hypothesis*, he refers to the work of economist Robert Frank, who once identified the difference between conspicuous and inconspicuous consumption. "Frank's explanation is simple: Conspicuous and inconspicuous consumption follow different psychological rules. Conspicuous consumption refers to the things that are visible to others and that are taken as a marker of a person's relative success. These goods are subject to a kind of arms race, where their value comes not so much from their objective properties as from the statement they make about their owner." Haidt then refers to Frank's understanding of inconspicuous consumption: "Inconspicuous consumption, on the other hand, refers to goods and activities that are valued for themselves, that are usually consumed more privately, and that are not bought for the purpose of achieving status."[21] Preachers are called to point out the futility of conspicuous consumption as a means of addressing spiritual hunger. It is a serious problem in North America, especially in affluent congregations.

This book will wrestle with one of the greatest tensions of our time: *proclaiming the message of Jesus Christ regarding money and possessions in an age of conspicuous consumption, in which the accumulation of wealth and possessions is glorified and coveted.* When reading the gospels, it becomes clear that Jesus had more to say about money and possessions than almost any other subject during his life and ministry. He knew they were a stumbling block in the first century, and they still are today.

Preachers who find themselves in affluent pulpits preaching to wealthy and powerful church members will certainly feel the tension when it comes to preaching and teaching about money. Many of the passages are incredibly challenging. Moreover, preachers who find themselves in poorer churches must find a way to give hope and comfort to those who are struggling to pay bills and make ends meet. All Christians, regardless of socioeconomic status, must wrestle with Jesus' teachings and parables. Simply avoiding the subject of money is not an option if we seek to be faithful to the gospel. Unfortunately, many will choose avoidance rather than faithfulness.

In some churches, money talk remains taboo, yet we live in a culture that is obsessed with money, driven by money, and focused on money. Money means power and influence, accomplishment and prestige. Money is often the way we judge the value of people and whether or not they have been successful in life. Money drives political passions, perspectives, and elections. The Great Recession brought the subject of money and materialism to the forefront, and it became an excellent teaching moment for preachers to focus on priorities and what really matters in life. The stock market plunged, banks went belly up, corruption scandals were unveiled, retirement accounts were cut in half, and millions of jobs were lost. Everybody was affected in one way or another, including churches and other charitable organizations that suffered financial consequences. The subject of money and possessions is timeless and relevant to all Christians.

Most churches have an annual stewardship campaign either in the fall or spring to raise commitments and funds for the church's operating budget. At our church, it usually happens in the spring immediately following Easter, with the new church year beginning on July 1. During the stewardship campaign, preachers will often focus on one of the many texts or parables that have to do with money. However, if this is the only time of the year that this happens, they are doing their congregation a great disservice. It then appears that we only preach and teach about money when the church needs it. But how we use our money throughout the year is a direct reflection of our spiritual lives and our values. I agree with Jim Wallis that bank statements and calendars are moral documents. To learn what is most important to a person, just look at the way that person spends his or her time and money. Money makes a great servant in life, but it can also make a terrible master. If we allow our money to serve us and the things that we want to support, that is good. But if we are enslaved to our money and to the accumulation of wealth and possessions, we will be miserable. The people in life who know best that money is not the secret to happiness are those who have plenty of it and yet remain restless and miserable. Some of the happiest and most joy-filled people in our world are those who have little or nothing and have learned to live simply.

Baylor University sociologists Paul Froese and Christopher Bader published a book in 2010 titled *America's Four Gods: What We Say About God and What That Says About Us.* The premise of the book is fairly straightforward: Americans generally believe in God but our concepts of God are very different. Froese and Bader focus on two primary questions. First, How engaged is God in the world? And, second, How judgmental is God? Their research indicates that there are four basic conceptions of God. The "Authoritative God" is both engaged in the world and judgmental. The "Benevolent God" is engaged but nonjudgmental. The "Critical God" is judgmental but disengaged. And the "Distant God" is nonjudgmental and disengaged.[22] In a chapter titled "God and Mammon," Froese and Bader say, "Overall, Americans tend to agree on two basic points: capitalism is good, and poverty is bad. How we reconcile a system that fosters inequality with an ethic to alleviate poverty is a function of what we think God wants from us. Social status plays a primary role in how we view God and his attitude about our economic system."[23]

Therefore, in an economically diverse congregation, there will be multiple perspectives as to what God expects, and there probably will not be a consensus on issues of money and politics. "At the end of the day, we are all 'values' and 'pocketbook' voters. In general, your values reflect your God and your God reflects your pocketbook. Lower economic status is strongly related to the belief that God harshly judges and is angry with the world. In turn, belief in a judgmental God (both Authoritative and Critical Gods) is related to the belief that the solution to poverty is personal faith or faith based solutions and not government intervention."[24] For Froese and Bader, theology, politics, and economics are clearly interconnected.

Money and Stewardship

The issue of money and stewardship is relevant to pastors, churches, and religious organizations because, as our culture has become more secular and materialistic, religious giving and financial support for the church has declined at an alarming rate. Christian Smith, Michael Emerson, and Patricia Smell published a book in 2008 titled *Passing the Plate: Why American Christians Don't Give Away More Money.* Their research was extensive, eye-opening, and in many ways disappointing for those concerned about the future of Christianity. In their chapter "Toward Explaining Ungenerous Giving," they offer nine hypotheses concerning why religious giving is less than generous. I simply wish to list them here because they are fascinating and well supported by research:

Hypothesis 1 – Objective Resource Constraints: Despite American Affluence generally, many American Christians simply do not possess the discretionary financial resources to give 10 percent of their income, given the many fixed costs of living in American society.

Hypothesis 2 – Subjective Resource Constraints: Many American Christians, whatever their objective financial capacities, subjectively believe they do not possess the financial resources to give 10 percent of their income.

Hypothesis 3 – Unperceived Needs: Most American Christians do not give their money generously because they simply do not perceive existing legitimate needs that their money could address and meet.

Hypothesis 4 – Normative Ignorance: Low levels of financial giving by American Christians are due in part to believers' simple lack of awareness that the faith traditions of most churches teach either 10 percent tithing or generous, sacrificial, proportionate financial giving as the norm of Christian stewardship.

Hypothesis 5 – Administrative Distrust: American Christians do not give their money generously because they are suspicious of waste and abuse by nonprofit administrators, especially those with access to too much surplus wealth.

Hypothesis 6 – Low Leadership Expectations: American Christians do not give generously because their churches hold low expectations of financial giving—insecure church leadership and congregational cultures oriented toward avoiding possible offense soft-peddle expectations of faithful, generous giving.

Hypothesis 7 – Collective Action Shirking: American Christians do not give money generously because they lack confidence that other American Christians are also contributing generously and do not want to be individually responsible for achieving collective goals.

Hypothesis 8 – Issue Privatization: Most American Christians do not give their money generously because matters of personal and family finances are highly privatized in American culture, effectively removing religious giving from any public discussion or accountability.

Hypothesis 9 – Non-Routine Giving Process: American Christians give relatively little money because much of their giving tends to be occasional and situational, not a consistent, structured, routine practice.[25]

I find Hypothesis 6—Low Leadership Expectations—most interesting for preachers. Many churches hold low giving expectations because the preachers and pastors are afraid to broach the subject. Preachers who are afraid to discuss stewardship expectations tend to stay away from money talk in general. But giving is a spiritual practice and an act of discipleship. Jesus made that abundantly clear. In an age of growing consumerism and materialism, the issue simply cannot be ignored.

The remaining chapters of this book we will wrestle with what it means to faithfully preach the gospel in a capitalistic culture that worships the "almighty dollar." I will focus specifically on the issues of money and materialism and what various scholars have to say about the subjects. Chapter 2 will identify some of Jesus' specific teachings and parables on money and materialism to indicate how these teachings challenge the prevailing mindset of North American culture. Chapter 3 will analyze the work of theological ethicist Stanley Hauerwas, who has spent his career critiquing Christian America and warning of the dangers of idolatry, consumerism, and blindly pursuing "The American Dream." Hauerwas is a pivotal figure in Christian ethics, and his voice is one we should hear. He sees greed as a spiritual condition that is a major stumbling block for American Christians. In chapter 4 we will look at the sermons and writings of United Methodist pastor Adam Hamilton, who does an excellent job of consistently addressing this issue within the mainline context of his congregation, The Church of the Resurrection, in Leawood, Kansas. Hamilton shows great courage and insight in his willingness to take on tough issues such as money and materialism in a politically diverse context. Lastly, I will provide a series of ten conclusions, building on the work of Hauerwas and Hamilton, to challenge preachers who faithfully preach and pastor in a restless culture that has become obsessed with money and is overly materialistic.

CHAPTER 2

* * * * * * * * * * * * * * * *

Jesus' Political and Economic Agenda

In 2011, I was preaching a sermon series on "Christianity and Capitalism," acknowledging the fact that tension exists between the two if we take the words of Jesus seriously. The two can and certainly do coexist in American culture, but I consider Christianity to be the conscience of capitalism in many ways. In between the two services on that particular Sunday, one of our associate ministers blindsided me with a question: "Do you think it's possible that there is tension between Christianity and capitalism because Jesus was a socialist?" To be honest, that question caught me off guard because the term socialism did not exist until the nineteenth century. However, the socialist mindset has always been present. I don't think Jesus was a socialist, but I would acknowledge that some of his teachings and parables have socialist overtones. It would be fascinating to hear Jesus' thoughts on modern-day capitalism and the free market.

Here is a perplexing question: "Was Jesus political?" The answer for many is a resounding "yes," which then leads to more questions: "What type of politics did he advocate, and what type of politics would he advocate today?" Would he be a Democrat? Would he be a Republican? Would he be independent? What would he think of the Tea Party? What would he think of Trump, Clinton, Cruz, or Sanders? Christian leaders on the political left and right claim to be the "true Christians." Jim Wallis is just as passionate about his views regarding poverty and war as Jerry Falwell once was regarding homosexuality and abortion. Since both can't be right on issues where they adamantly disagree, whom should we believe?

Of the four gospels, Luke is the one quoted most often when talking about the politics of Jesus. At the very beginning of Jesus' ministry, following his time spent alone in the wilderness, Luke tells us that Jesus was in Nazareth and he went to the synagogue to teach on the Sabbath. Then he says:

[T]he scroll of the prophet Isaiah was given to him. He unrolled the scroll and found the place where it was written:

"The Spirit of the Lord is upon me,
    because he has anointed me
    to bring *good news to the poor.*
He has sent me to proclaim release to the captives
    and recovery of sight to the blind,
    to let the oppressed go free,
    to proclaim the year of the Lord's favor."
    (emphasis added by author)

According to Luke, Jesus goes on to say, "Today this scripture has been fulfilled in your hearing."[1] Many view this as the basic platform and agenda for Jesus' life and ministry. Luke seems to be acknowledging that this is indeed what Jesus came to do, and there are certainly political and economic ramifications to these words.

Luke's Account

In his groundbreaking book *The Politics of Jesus,* Notre Dame theologian and ethicist John Howard Yoder says that with these words in Luke's Gospel, "Jesus was announcing the imminent implementation of a new regime whose marks would be that the rich would give to the poor, the captives would be freed, and the hearers would have a new mentality (*metanoia*), if they believed this news."[2] Yoder acknowledges that the words "today, this scripture has been fulfilled" are somewhat ambiguous as to timing and place. We do not know if Jesus was referring to a future event or to an unfolding series of events that were about to start. However, Yoder emphatically argues that we do know this: "It is a visible socio-political, economic restructuring of relations among the people of God, achieved by divine intervention in the person of Jesus as the one anointed and endued with the spirit."[3] Yoder leaves little doubt that these opening words of Jesus in Luke's Gospel have both political and economic significance.

In answering the question, "Was Jesus political?" Yoder believes it is important to look at how the political authorities of his day responded to his rise in popularity. "Both Jewish and Roman authorities were defending themselves against a real threat. That the threat was not one of *armed,* violent revolt, and that it nonetheless bothered them to the point of their resorting to irregular procedures to counter it, is a proof of the political relevance of nonviolent tactics, not a proof that Pilate and Caiaphas were exceptionally dull or dishonorable men."[4] Simply reading the gospels will show that the authorities of the day were very clearly worried about Jesus, his popularity, and the Kingdom that he proclaimed. Harvard theologian Harvey Cox echoes this sentiment in his book *When Jesus Came to Harvard:* "The Romans had already made Herod King of the Jews, so if this upstart Rabbi had royal pretensions, and since he seemed to be gathering a popular following, this was a clear and present danger to Roman rule."[5] The gospels attest that Jesus was arrested and then put to death because he was viewed by the authorities of his day as a political threat. If he had not been viewed as a threat, the events of Holy Week would not have unfolded the way they did. Jesus was executed for a reason.

Yoder's *The Politics of Jesus* continues to be viewed by many scholars as a new beginning in the study of Jesus and politics in the twentieth (and now the twenty-first) century. His careful analysis of Luke's Gospel and the implications of what Jesus claimed to be the platform of his ministry cannot be overlooked. Yoder concludes the second chapter of his book, "The Kingdom Coming," by saying:

> Jesus was not just a moralist whose teachings had some
> political implications; he was not primarily a teacher
> of spirituality whose public ministry unfortunately was

seen in a political light; he was not just a sacrificial lamb preparing for his immolation, or a God-man whose divine status calls us to disregard his humanity. Jesus was, in his divinely mandated (i.e., promised, anointed, messianic) prophethood, priesthood, and kingship, the bearer of a new possibility of human, social, and therefore political relationships. His baptism is the inauguration and his cross is the culmination of that new regime in which his disciples are called to share. Hearers or readers may choose to consider that kingdom as not real, or not relevant, or not possible, or not inviting; but no longer can we come to this choice in the name of systematic theology or honest hermeneutics.[6]

So, that begs the question: Why do so many today disagree with Yoder and continue to believe that Jesus was nonpolitical? Are they in denial? Is it because Jesus does not accommodate their particular politics? Or do they simply seek to maintain a clear separation between personal faith and spirituality and the way that faith manifests itself in society? Yoder seems to have little patience for those who want to maintain this separation. For him, Jesus' message was a socio-political kingdom then, and still is today.

Like Yoder, I too believe that Jesus was political, and the best place for us to look in order to understand his politics is the gospels. However, it is important to remember that he proclaimed a different kind of *Kingdom,* and partisan relevance for today is not as clear as some might like to believe. No one political party has a monopoly on Jesus' agenda. There are a few other passages of scripture that give us a clear glimpse into Jesus' passion and agenda. To be consistent, I want to follow Yoder's lead and stick with Luke's Gospel. The biblical commentary of the British Bible scholar William Barclay (whose words I have always found most helpful in the process of sermon preparation and exegesis) also provides insight. I am also drawing on commentary by New Testament scholars William Brosend, Richard Lischer, and Amy Jill Levine.

In Luke 6, we find the "Sermon on the Plain." There Jesus says:

"Blessed are you who are poor,
for yours is the kingdom of God.
Blessed are you who are hungry now,
for you will be filled.
Blessed are you who weep now,
for you will laugh.

Blessed are you when people hate you, and when
they exclude you, revile you, and defame you on
account of the Son of Man. Rejoice in that day and
leap for joy, for surely your reward is great in heaven;
for that is what their ancestors did to the prophets.

But woe to you who are rich,
for you have received your consolation.
Woe to you who are full now,
for you will be hungry.
Woe to you who are laughing now,
for you will mourn and weep.
Woe to you when all speak well of you, for that is
what their ancestors did to the false prophets."[7]

These words may have come as a shock for those listening
in the first century, especially to the rich. In his commentary
on these verses, Barclay says, "They take the accepted standards
and turn them upside down. The people whom Jesus called
happy the world called wretched; and the people Jesus called
wretched, the world would call happy. Just imagine anyone
saying 'Happy are the poor, and Woe to the rich!' To talk like
that is to put an end to the world's values altogether."[8] Jesus is
taking the common perceptions of the world about wealth and
money and turning them upside down. His comments turned
heads in first-century Palestine and they still turn heads today.

If we look ahead in the Sermon on the Plain, the challenge
continues. We find Jesus saying this about enemies and
retaliation:

"But I say to you that listen, Love your enemies, do
good to those who hate you, bless those who curse you,
pray for those who abuse you. If anyone strikes you on

the cheek, offer the other also; and from anyone who takes away your coat do not withhold even your shirt. Give to everyone who begs from you; and if anyone takes away your goods, do not ask for them again. Do to others as you would have them do to you. If you love those who love you, what credit is that to you? For even sinners love those who love them. If you do good to those who do good to you, what credit is that to you? For even sinners do the same. If you lend to those from whom you hope to receive, what credit is that to you? Even sinners lend to sinners, to receive as much again. But love your enemies, do good, and lend, expecting nothing in return. Your reward will be great, and you will be children of the Most High; for he is kind to the ungrateful and the wicked. Be merciful, just as your Father is merciful.[9]

Some say that Jesus is setting forth an impossible living standard that no human being could ever attain. Perhaps this is true, and maybe it is an ideal that we should always strive for as opposed to a reality that we reach.

On September 11, 2011, the ten-year anniversary of September 11, which happened to fall on a Sunday, the lectionary text was on forgiveness. Forgiveness! I remember thinking to myself while preparing the sermon, "Who wants to hear about forgiveness on September 11?" That is an example of the challenge that lies before Christians who want to take the words of Jesus seriously and at face value. Jesus is calling us to move beyond what may be our natural tendency or emotion to a much more challenging yet worthy proposition. Barclay says, "There is no commandment of Jesus which has caused so much discussion and debate as the commandment to love our enemies."[10] In the twenty-first–century world of terrorism, nuclear weapons, and potential mass destruction, this standard becomes all the more challenging.

From Luke's Sermon on the Plain, we can make some initial conclusions about the politics of Jesus. He was an advocate for the poor and the hungry. He cared for those who were sad and shared in their plight. He stood firm with those who were persecuted for being his followers. He was wary of systems that favored the rich while taking advantage of the poor. He challenged his followers to love their enemies, pray for their persecutors, turn the other cheek, and treat others the way they would want to be treated. He opened up the possibility that God's Kingdom will look nothing like the kingdoms of this world.

Jesus' Use of Parables

Jesus taught in parables too. In his book *Conversations with Scripture: The Parables,* New Testament scholar William Brosend affirms British scholar C. H. Dodd's definition of a parable: "At its simplest, a parable is a metaphor or simile, drawn from nature or the common life, arresting the hearer by its vividness or strangeness, and leaving the mind in sufficient doubt about its precise application to tease it into active thought."[11] Jesus used ordinary examples of his day to illustrate extraordinary truths about the Kingdom of God. The parables also shed light on his political and economic worldview.

In Luke 10:25–37, we find the parable of the good Samaritan. This is perhaps the best known of all the parables, yet it is unique to Luke's Gospel. In response to Jesus' question as to what it written in the law, the lawyer gives what is known as the greatest and second commandments: "Love the Lord your God with all your heart, and with all your soul, and with all your strength, and with all your mind; and love your neighbor as yourself."[12] In response to the lawyer's question, "who is my neighbor?" Jesus tells this story. It was not the pious priest or the Levite who stopped to help the man beaten by robbers; it was the Samaritan. In the first century, the Jews had little to do with the Samaritans. They did not associate with them, and so the fact that Jesus makes the Samaritan the hero in this story must have been alarming. This shows that Jesus was not into the stereotyping or profiling of that day. He sought to break down barriers of class and nationality while challenging his followers to stop and help those in need regardless of who they may be. The parable of the good Samaritan is a reminder that, every day, life presents itself with opportunities to help those in need. We can either hurry by in our busy state, or we can take the time to show compassion and to do the will of God. Jesus says that any person in need is our neighbor. It is probably true that the priest and Levite in this story had compassion for the man, but they did not act on that compassion. It is possible to feel sorry for others but then do nothing about their misery or misfortune. Jesus' challenge is to always stop and help those in need regardless of who they may be.

Brosend offers the following insights on the parable of the good Samaritan:

> No matter our opinion about the legal profession, we find ourselves identifying with the lawyer, and see the example of the Samaritan being the example we are to follow. No, we don't stop every time we see an injured person in the road, but we read the story from the perspective of one having the power to do so if we choose. The force of the story therefore is taken as an encouragement to choose to help more often. That is a good Christian attitude. We are the ones who can make a difference—change the world, even—if only we would decide to do so.[13]

Changing the world and making a difference can only happen after one makes the decision to help. Brosend illustrates what set the Samaritan apart from the other two travelers: "Unlike the priest and Levite, the Samaritan stopped. He stopped. Wherever he was going, whatever he was doing, however big a hurry he was in, he stopped. And then, because he was willing to stop, he could see the situation for what it was, and realized that the fellow in the ditch was injured, not dead, and when he took in the situation, he was 'moved with pity' (Luke 10:33)."[14] It is possible to see the great need in the world, to acknowledge it, but never stop to do anything about it. This happens all the time.

In Luke 12:13–21, we find the parable of the rich fool. Jesus tells the story about a man whose crops produced abundantly, and he decides to build larger barns to store his grain and goods. An initial reading of this parable might lead one to believe that Jesus has it out for rich people. However, there is more to this story. Brosend remarks, "What makes the man foolish is not what he did and said, but the attitude that was at the root of his decision-making process. He decided as one who lived only for himself and thought that he would live indefinitely." Jesus refers to this man as a "fool" because of his mindset. "It's not that rich people will die and poor people will not; it is that rich people sometimes have a way of living as if they think they will never die. But they will, and if they wait until then to discover that 'life does not consist in the abundance of possessions' (Luke 12:15), it will be too late in all kinds of ways."[15] The danger of excessive hoarding is the false presumption that life will never end.

New Testament scholar Richard Lischer says this about Jesus' mindset regarding the rich fool in this parable: "There is no mystery here: this is precisely the sort of person you should *not* become, and exactly the foolish behavior you should avoid at all costs."[16] In this parable, Jesus is forcing us to wrestle with the way that we define meaning and significance in life. Brosend states, "What is being required of us is not just our biological life (Greek *zoe*), but the very principal that makes us alive, our soul (Greek *psuche*). Our life 'consists' in our relationship to God, for us as Christians a relationship defined through Jesus Christ. Everything else, in life and death, flows from and through that or it is less than it might be and will stop with our death."[17] Jesus' statement in this parable, "One's life does not consist in the abundance of possessions,"[18] can be directly tied to his claim in the Sermon on the Mount: "Do not store up for yourself treasures on earth, where moth and rust consume and where thieves break in and steal; but store up for yourselves treasures in heaven" (Mt. 6:19–20a). Jesus seeks to break us from our attachment to possessions so that we may find deeper meaning in life.

In Luke 14:16–24, we find another parable that gives us a glimpse into the mind of Jesus—the parable of the great dinner. Jesus had just finished teaching about humility and hospitality. Once again, we see Jesus identifying with the poor and the outcasts of society and saying that they are welcome in the Kingdom. What is the basic message here? Barclay argues, "In the parable, the master stands for God. Throughout all their history they had looked forward to the day when God would break in; and when he did, they tragically refused his invitation. The poor people from the streets and lanes stand for the tax-gatherers and sinners who welcomed Jesus in ways the orthodox never did."[19] In that day, there were many Jews who were simply too busy to hear the message of Jesus about the Kingdom. In our world today, especially among the affluent, there is every reason under the sun as to why one is too busy to respond to Jesus' call. Barclay continues: "It often happens that when people enter into new possessions they become so taken up with them that the claims of worship and God get crowded out."[20] There will always be factors distracting us from the Kingdom of God, but Jesus is not interested in hearing those. He is interested in those who are ready and willing to come to the banquet that has been prepared, regardless of their class or socioeconomic status.

Brosend makes the connection between the message of this parable and the words of the prophet Isaiah (quoted in Luke 4) in referring to those who end up being invited to the dinner.

> Closer to hand, these are among those people whom Isaiah (61:1–2), and Jesus in reading Isaiah and affirming the fulfillment of the Scripture, have embraced. "The spirit of the Lord is upon me, because he has anointed me to bring good news to the poor. He has sent me to proclaim release to the captives and recovery of sight to the blind, to let the oppressed go free, to proclaim the year of the Lord's favor" (Luke 4:18–19). For the one giving the banquet to command his slave to bring in those usually thought to be cast out is remarkable in every way.[21]

With this parable, Jesus continues to demonstrate how Isaiah's words regarding the poor and the marginalized matter. Hospitality is important, and so is responding to God's invitation. As Brosend points out, "The caution is not to presume upon position. You think your seat is reserved, but if you do not respond when told, 'Come for everything is ready now,' you may be in for a surprise. When it comes to the Kingdom of God, matters of timing are not up to us."[22]

The Events of Holy Week

In Luke 19, Holy Week begins with Jesus' triumphal entry into Jerusalem. When we take the time to think of the difference between Jesus' humble procession versus the ostentatious procession of Pilate, we can begin to see how this is symbolic of his Kingdom and how it differs from the kingdoms of this world. The crowds cheered and waved palm branches as he humbly rode into Jerusalem on a donkey, thus fulfilling the words of the Prophet Zechariah.

Immediately following this event, Luke tells of how Jesus weeps for Jerusalem and then cleanses the temple, which gives us great insight into his views about the money-changers and financial exploitation of the poor. Luke says:

> Then he entered the temple and began to drive out those who were selling things there; and he said, "It is written,
> 'My house shall be a house of prayer';
> but you have made it a den of robbers."

> Every day he was teaching in the temple. The chief priests, the scribes, and the leaders of the people kept looking for a way to kill him; but they did not find anything they could do, for all the people were spellbound by what they heard.[23]

This is one of the select times in the gospels when we find Jesus angry, and he acts out in anger in a very public manner. Every male Jew in the first century had to pay a temple tax of roughly one half of a shekel, which was equal to roughly two days of labor for a peasant or a member of the working class. Money-changers were notorious for making a profit, especially during the Passover, and Jesus was fed up. The poor were being exploited. Barclay says: "Jesus cleansed the Temple with such violence because its traffic was being used to exploit helpless men and women. It was not simply that the buying and selling interfered with the dignity and solemnity of worship; it was that the very worship of the house of God was being used to exploit the worshippers. It was the passion for social justice which burned in Jesus' heart when he took this drastic step."[24]

Almost every empire in the history of civilization has been guilty of exploiting the poor and working class to benefit the wealthy. Just as in this case, it is done in a systematic way through the imposition of taxes that are mandated by law and are not optional. Jesus was certainly aware that this was happening, and what made it worse was that it was happening in the temple, the house of God, and being imposed by the religious rulers of that day. This still happens in our world today. The poor are often exploited to benefit the rich, and most of the time few possess the courage or ability to challenge the system. Systemic injustice is the most difficult to confront because it does not have a face. Many are comfortable simply saying, "That is the way it is," but that certainly does not make it right. Jesus had the courage and audacity to speak out against this and still challenges his followers to do the same. The cleansing of the temple is a reminder that there comes a point when enough is enough, and we are called to speak out on behalf of the poor and the powerless.

In Luke 20, Jesus is asked a question that is intended to trap him or to be a trick question: "Teacher, we know that you are right in what you say and teach, and you show deference to no one, but teach the way of God in accordance with truth. Is it lawful for us to pay taxes to the emperor, or not?"[25] Luke tells us that Jesus sensed the trickery and craftiness of the question. He gives the following answer: "'Show me a denarius. Whose head and whose title does it bear?' They said, 'The emperor's.' He said to them, 'Then give to the emperor the things that are the emperor's, and give to God the things that are God's.'"[26] Jesus' clever response stops them in their tracks. If Jesus had said that taxes should not be paid, they would have turned him in to Pilate and had him immediately arrested. If he said the taxes should be paid, he may have disappointed many of his followers. Barclay's commentary is again helpful here:

(i) If a man lives in a state and enjoys all of its privileges, he cannot divorce himself from it. The more honest a man is, the better citizen he will be. There should be no better and no more conscientious citizens of any state than its Christians; and one of the tragedies of modern life is that Christians do not sufficiently take their part in the government of the state. If they abandon their responsibilities and leave materialistic politicians to govern, Christians cannot justifiably complain about what is done or not done.

(ii) Nonetheless, it remains true that in the life of the Christian God has the last word and not the state. The voice of conscience is louder than the voice of any man-made laws. The Christian is at once the servant and the conscience of the state. Just because he is the best of citizens, he will refuse to do what a Christian citizen cannot do. He will at once and the same time fear God and honor the king.[27]

According to Jesus, it is possible to serve God and still be a loyal citizen of the state. However, if the two ever contradict each other, the Christian is first and foremost accountable to God. Typically, in America at least, this choice does not have to be made. However, it is still the responsibility of the Christian to be involved in government and to speak out in the face of injustice and oppression.

Finally, we turn to the end of Luke's Gospel, where Jesus has been betrayed by Judas, denied by Peter, arrested, mocked, beaten, taken before Pilate and Herod, and then sentenced to crucifixion—the most brutal of deaths. Luke adds to this his account of Jesus' resurrection (Lk. 23:32–47). It is difficult to gain a clear understanding of Jesus' agenda without understanding his final days on earth and how his life came to a violent end. The politics of Jesus led him to death by execution because he was viewed as a threat to the authorities. If he had not been viewed as a political and economic threat, he would not have been put to death.[28] Yoder makes this point time and time again in *The Politics of Jesus*. To understand the life and politics of Jesus we have to first understand what led him to the cross. "The cross of Christ was not an inexplicable or chance event, which happened to strike him, like illness or accident. To accept the cross as his destiny, to move toward it and even to provoke it, when he could well have done otherwise, was Jesus' constantly reiterated free choice."[29]

Many today have a hard time accepting that the way of Jesus is the way of the cross. Many look past Good Friday and want nothing to do with confrontation or with suffering, but these things are intertwined into the gospel story. Yoder later continues: "The cross of Calvary was not a difficult family situation, not a frustration of visions of personal fulfillment, a crushing debt, or a nagging in-law; it was the political, legally-to-be-expected result of a moral clash with the powers ruling his society."[30] Jesus came face to face with the power structure, and the powerful put him to death. However, Jesus knew exactly what he was doing and what his fate would be. God sent Jesus into the world to teach us how to love and treat each other, and the world put him to death.

In the book *The Last Week: What the Gospels Really Teach about Jesus' Final Days in Jerusalem,* biblical scholars Marcus Borg and John Dominic Crossan provide helpful insight into the political implications of the cross, and, in many ways, they affirm Yoder's position. Using Mark's Gospel as their guiding text, they give the following understanding of Good Friday: "The execution of Jesus was virtually inevitable. Not because of divine necessity, but because of human inevitability—this is what domination systems did to people who publicly and vigorously challenged them."[31] Borg and Crossan are attempting to answer the question: "Did Good Friday have to happen? As divine necessity? No. As human inevitability? Virtually. Good Friday is the result of the collision between the passion of Jesus and the domination system of his time."[32] Jesus had been viewed as a threat to the Roman Empire. The only problem: He was not striving to overthrow the government. He was simply speaking out in a courageous yet nonviolent manner against an unfair political system. The result was his public execution on a cross.

Matthew's Account

Turning to Matthew's Gospel, we find additional passages that give us helpful insight into the way Jesus viewed money and possessions. In 19:16–26, we find the story of the rich man. Preachers who pastor more affluent churches are often guilty of overlooking this text. Why? Well, consider what Jesus says in verse 24: "It is easier for a camel to go through the eye of a needle than for someone who is rich to enter the kingdom of God." It is understandable why these words would make a wealthy person uncomfortable. What did Jesus mean? It was clear in this situation that the rich man had kept all of the laws and commandments since his youth. It was also clear to Jesus that he was completely attached to, obsessed with, and defined by his possessions. He did not know how to exist apart from them. So what does Jesus do? He challenges the man to get rid of all that he owns because that is the only way he is going to enter the kingdom of God. Again, Jesus is not saying that having wealth and possessions is bad in and of itself. But if we become so attached that we cannot exist apart from them, it then becomes necessary to get rid of them. We cannot allow money and material things to define us. The rich man was unable to do this, so he went away sad.

In chapter 22, we find Matthew's account of Jesus being asked whether or not it is lawful to pay taxes to the emperor. The context of this passage makes it clear that an attempt is being made to trap Jesus and test him. As in many other situations, Jesus was able to creatively think outside of the box and provide a wise and profound answer to a trick question. Amy Jill Levine, New Testament scholar at Vanderbilt University, while speaking to the Downtown Rotary Club of Nashville in July of 2012, referred to the brilliance of Jesus' response to this question posed by the Pharisees. Here is a significant portion of her remarks on this passage:

1.   First, the question itself, "Should we pay taxes or not?" is designed to "trap" Jesus. It is, in his own context, an impossible question. If he says, "Yes, pay your taxes," the majority of the people in Judea, living under Roman occupation, would immediately reject him. They would no more want to pay taxes to Rome than the American colonists wanted to pay taxes to the British king. However, if he says, "No, do not pay," then the

Roman soldiers occupying the city would arrest him immediately as a seditionist.

2. Second, Jesus does not actually say, "Pay your taxes." Instead, he begins by saying, "Why are you putting me to the test?" That verse is often overlooked, but it should not be. The term "test" (in Greek, the language in which the NT is written) can also be translated "tempt." The famous prayer known as the "Our Father" has the line, "Lead us not into temptation"—the line reads literally, "Do not bring us to the test." We can extend: do not test people by asking for sound bites about the very complicated question of taxes. People of good will, and good minds, may well have very different, and nuanced views. The conversation is not simple.

3. Third, that same term, "test" or "tempt," shows up elsewhere in the Gospels to describe what Satan does to Jesus—he tempts or tests Jesus with an offer of political expedience: worship me, says Satan, and you can have all the kingdoms of the world. Jesus declines: his interest is not in political power, but, as he puts it, "Worship the Lord your God, and serve only him" (Mt. 4:10). Discussion of taxes should not be put forward to score political gain; it should be put forward for what is good for the nation.

4. Fourth, Jesus then says, "Bring me a denarius and let me see it." Apparently, Jesus has no coin of his own. He is not among the wealthy, and among his major concerns is care for the poor. As he puts it, "Again I tell you, it is easier for a camel to go through the eye of a needle than for someone who is rich to enter the kingdom of God" (Mt. 19:24).

Contrary to popular wisdom, there is no "camel's gate" in Jerusalem through which camels passed, albeit with difficulty. The statement is hyperbole; Jesus is exaggerating. That was a popular rhetorical form of the time, and it was designed to catch the attention of the listener. His point is that the rich should use their resources to help care for the poor, because, as he states, quoting the book of Leviticus, "You should love your neighbor as yourself."

5. Finally, he responds, "Give to the emperor the things that are the emperor's, and to God the things that are God's." The answer is not a directive; it is a challenge. It is up to his audience to determine what belongs to God and what belongs to the state. If we think that the state deserves funding, we pay it. If we think that everything belongs to God, then we might consider a tax protest. The point is that we are to think, seriously, about what we want to do with our money, about how we see it being used by those in authority, and about how we understand our money in relation to our moral and religious values.[33]

Levine demonstrates how Jesus finds a way to put the ball back in the court of the Pharisees. He refused to be trapped.

Christians must still decide today what belongs to the "emperor" and what belongs to God. It is clear that the debate about taxes, tax codes, tax burdens, and allegiance to the empire continues to be one of the most heated in our day and age. What does God require? What does Caesar require? To which are we most loyal?

Lastly, let us turn to Matthew 25. Beginning in verse 14, we find the parable of the talents. In summary, a man is going on a journey, so he summons his slaves and gives each of them a different number of talents. To the first he gives five talents, to the second he gives two, and to the third he gives one. When he returns, he calls the slaves to come and settle the accounts. The one to whom he gave five has gone and made five more. The one to whom he gave two has made two more. But the slave who received just one talent took it and hid it in the ground out of fear of losing it. The owner is angry and blasts the slave for not putting his talent to use. He then takes the one talent and gives it to the slave who has ten.[34]

What is the lesson of this parable? One response is that Jesus makes it clear that God is less concerned with what we have and more concerned with if and how we use it. This is true with our money and our abilities. According to Brosend, we should learn a great lesson from the third servant: "It seems we need to pay attention to what we are doing with what we've got."[35] Time and resources are not to be hoarded but used to help others and glorify God. Richard Lischer argues: "This is not a happy story. It is a cautionary tale addressed to those entrusted with the Lord's work, but who lack the courage to embrace its inherent value for the purposes of growth in the kingdom of heaven."[36] Both Brosend and Lischer point out that many churches use this parable for stewardship purposes, but the lesson is far greater and extends beyond raising money for the church. Lischer contends, "The 'talents' do not denote our peculiar abilities or resources but refer to dispensations of grace that belong to God and come only from God. What is being invested is not *my* money, *my* valuable time, or *my* extraordinary expertise, but the generously bestowed blessings of God."[37] Given this mindset, life itself is an act of generosity and stewardship.

Matthew continues this message in the following passage, commonly referred to as the "Judgment of the Nations." Jesus says, "Truly I tell you, just as you did it to one of the least of these who are members of my family, you did it to me."[38] Once again, Jesus seems less concerned with what we have and more concerned with whether we use it to help others, especially those who are cast aside by the world. This is similar to the message found in the parable of the good Samaritan (Luke 10), in which it was not the priest or the Levite who did the will of God; it was the Samaritan who stopped and helped the man beaten by robbers and left on the side of the road. It is possible in life to have compassion for those who are in need but not to act on that compassion. The genuine test of faith is whether or not we have helped those who are struggling and who the world is passing by—those who are hungry, naked, homeless, sick, or in prison.

From looking at these passages in both Luke and Matthew's Gospels, we can see that Jesus held passionate views regarding money, possessions, compassion, and generosity. He felt that one should not be defined by the accumulation of wealth and possessions, but should use resources to help others who are in need. Excess and hoarding continue to be problems in our age.

It is easy to develop the mindset that enough is never enough. Greed and selfishness are destructive paths and completely work against the politics of Jesus. Capitalism must be kept in check by the words and teachings of Jesus that advocate compassion and generosity. Jesus is challenging us to go out of our way to help others, and that involves both money and time. Christians must be willing to have open and honest conversations about how we view money and possessions in light of Christ's teachings. Preachers are called to boldly address this topic.

We will now turn to an academic ethicist who has faithfully addressed this subject in his research and teaching.

CHAPTER 3

* * * * * * * * * * * * * *

Stanley Hauerwas on Greed, Desire, and Possessions

Preachers are sometimes hesitant to follow Jesus' lead in addressing the subject of greed. Greed is a problem in any capitalistic society on every socioeconomic level. In Luke 12, Jesus said, "Take care! Be on your guard against all types of greed; for one's life does not consist in the abundance of possessions."[1] How well does that verse go over at an Ivy League business school full of ambitious MBA students? How well does that verse go over at a Wall Street cocktail party? The problem with greed is that nobody thinks they are being greedy because there is always somebody who has more. It is always others who are greedy. Wealth seems relative.

Duke theologian Stanley Hauerwas has been on the forefront of Christian ethics for decades now. In 2001, *Time* magazine named him America's most influential theologian, an honor that gave him mixed emotions. Hauerwas has never been afraid to speak his mind, and he is best known for his passionate stance as a pacifist. However, he has also written extensively about greed, desire, and the dark side of capitalism. I believe he has some insights, analysis, and assessments we as ministers can learn much from on these matters, so I want to spend the bulk of this chapter unpacking his viewpoint. With that before us, I will then offer some caveats on Hauerwas' argument. We can definitely learn from him. At the same time, I do not think that adopting his views wholesale is the answer we need.

Hauerwas' View

In an article he wrote for *Religion and Ethics,* Hauerwas says, "For surely if any one characteristic is to be associated with greed, it is the presumption that no matter how much we may have we need 'more.' We need more because we cannot be sure that what we have is secure. So the more we have the more we must have in order to secure what we have."[2] Hauerwas believes that, in many ways, greed has become a given in America's economic system: "This brings us to an inescapable problem. Even if greed was once a primal sin, hasn't greed become necessary to sustain economic growth? In other words, we are obligated to want more because if we do not want more then we will put someone out of a job. That is the logic behind government stimulus."[3] As Americans, we live in a culture that conditions us to never be satisfied and to always want more.

Hauerwas acknowledges that many Christians say that God will provide, but they live as though security comes only through possessions and accumulation. He concludes the article by saying:

> Greed is thus rightly called a deadly sin because it perverts the possibility of a proper human relation to the Creator, from whom we have received all that we need as gift. Greed presumes and perpetuates a world of scarcity and want—a world in which there is never "enough." But a world shaped by scarcity is a world that cannot trust that God has given all that we need. Greed, in other words, prohibits faith. But the inverse is also true. For it is in the Christian celebration of the Eucharist that we have the prismatic act that makes possible our recognition that God has given us everything we need. The Eucharist not only is the proclamation of abundance, but it is the enactment of abundance. In the Eucharist we discover that we cannot use Christ up. In the Eucharist we discover that the more the body and blood of Christ is shared, the more there is to be shared. The Eucharist, therefore, is the way the Christian Church learns to understand why

generosity rather than greed can and must shape our economic relations.[4]

For Hauerwas, the Eucharist is a central reminder for Christians that God has given us enough in Christ, and we are called to resist greed and be a generous people.

Hauerwas and his colleague Will Willimon co-authored a book in 1999 titled *The Truth About God: The Ten Commandments in Christian Life*. The final chapter of that book is both powerful and provocative. It deals with the ninth and tenth commandments that have to do with coveting, and they point to the problem of desire in our culture: "Desire is contagious. We desire according to the desires of another because all desire is imitative. I want this or that because somebody else wants this or that. That we learn desire from one another means that we desperately desire one another's approval, even though our desires put us in envious conflicts with one another."[5]

Learning to tame our desire is a spiritual task in an age in which competition and social comparison seem to be the order of the day. In this new age of social media, everybody is aware of what others have and what they are doing. Competition and comparison are constant and ever present. "We think we deserve what our neighbour has, and anything our neighbour has that we do not have diminishes us. The socialist calls capitalism 'legalized greed,' and the capitalist calls socialism 'legalized envy,' and both have truth in what they say."[6] Capitalism has been referred to as the "worst economic system if it weren't for all the others." Its obvious benefits are rewarding hard work, initiative, creativity, and education. The conservative argument is that when those at the top do well, all boats rise. But the dark side of capitalism is greed, lack of regulation, and an enormous gap between the "haves" and the "have nots." We now live in an age where the top 1 percent control an unprecedented level of the world's wealth. Regardless, this is the economic system of the United States and therefore the living reality of those sitting in the pews. I have referred to Christianity before as the "conscience of capitalism," and I think for followers of Christ that should be true. Success is fine, but only if balanced by compassion and generosity.

We live in a culture of consumerism, so that is the culture to which we preach. And, in that culture, many people view the church and Christianity as something to be consumed, always asking the question, "What can the church do for me?" "How can the church meet my needs?" We also live in a culture of competition and comparison. Hauerwas and Willimon say, "We think of life as a zero sum game. Accordingly, we want what our neighbour has and we are led to an endless cycle of acquisition that never satisfies. American consumptive habits fuelled by capitalism are but the most obvious form of this behavior. We think our lives will be less if we don't have 'the latest,' but then we discover that the latest becomes dated almost before we get it home."[7] Finding fulfilment in material goods is always short lived. "Our problem as humans is not that we are full of desire, aflame with unfulfillment. Our problem is that we long for that which is unfulfilling. We attempt to be content with that which can never satisfy. As C.S. Lewis once said, we are far too easily pleased."[8] Material consumption of goods and services generally does not satisfy the soul, and, if it does, it is only for a short while. The question then becomes, "How should preachers challenge Christians to live in a world of consumption and materialism and not fall victim to the ongoing temptation to consume?" Better yet, how can we learn to focus on the spiritual and that which satisfies our deepest desires? How can we avoid the materialistic rat race? How can we keep ourselves from falling victim to the mindset that all we need is "a little bit more"?

Materialism runs rampant in our culture because success seems to be measured by bank accounts and possessions that serve as living scoreboards. Affluence seems to be marked by purchasing power and what we can accumulate. Self-worth is often measured by net worth. Again, Hauerwas and Willimon are on it:

A recent PBS documentary calls our sickness "affluenza" but we, being suspicious of the world's new words, prefer greed. It's sin, not sickness. The problem is that, in the world in which we live, we have learned to call greed "ambition" or "providing for my family." We have learned to call greed "getting ahead." We have learned to call greed "working for a better life." We have learned to call greed "pleasure." As Calvin put it, we have managed to blacken our mirrors so that we no longer see ourselves.[9]

Many will read these words of Hauerwas and Willimon and disagree. Where is the line drawn between working hard, providing for family, and becoming greedy? After all, was not our country built on the concept of the American dream: that if you work hard you can achieve success and enjoy the fruits of your labor? When did this become greed? Does not every generation hope to give the next generation a better life? And who is the judge of what constitutes greed and what constitutes responsible planning? Cost of living is expensive in many places. Sending your children to a school such as Duke University (where Hauerwas and Willimon teach) costs a lot. Is it greedy to save and plan for that? There is certainly not a consensus as to what constitutes greed.

Still, Hauerwas and Willimon are adamant that greed is a spiritual problem, and not only that but that greed is usually not hidden and is on public display: "The good thing about greed is that unlike some sin, it is not subtle. Its results are public, there for all to see. Accumulation tends toward conspicuous display. If we cannot show others what we have accumulated, what's the good of accumulation?"[10] From name brand clothes to jewelry, from expensive shoes to handbags, from luxury cars to mansions, everything we purchase in life sends a message of who we are, how much we have, and what is most important to us. And, for whatever reason, status is typically tied to money rather than personality, integrity, or character. Why? Because we are a materialistic society. We are a consumer culture. We have set up the game this way. This is where preaching to an affluent congregation becomes challenging.

- What does it say about somebody's priorities if they spend more money on country club dues in a month than they give to the church in a year?

- What does it say about somebody's priorities if they drop $250 at dinner on Saturday night and then place a $5 bill in the offering plate Sunday morning?

- What does it say about somebody's priorities if they buy a new pair of shoes at Nordstroms for $500 dollars but never support the church or any charity?

These are profound questions, and many people simply don't want to wrestle with them. These questions make for awkward conversations. Jesus told the rich young ruler that he must sell everything that he owned and give the money to the poor. The reason? His possessions were defining him. He simply could not imagine life without them. You might say that his possessions "possessed" him. As a pastor, I often wonder, "How many of those who sit in our pews define themselves by what they own? How many are held captive to the materialistic rat race?" Self-worth and net worth are not the same.

The capitalist will come back and say that envy is the real problem in our culture. There was a controversial article that appeared in *The New York Times* on March 1, 2014, titled "The Downside of Inciting Envy." Written by Arthur Brooks of the American Enterprise Institute, the article states that there is growing envy in our nation, and he explains why it is unhealthy. Brooks states: "Unsurprisingly, psychologists have found that envy pushes down life satisfaction and depresses well-being. Envy is positively correlated with depression and neuroticism, and the hostility it breeds may actually make us sick. Recent work suggests that envy can help explain our complicated relationship with social media: it often leads to destructive 'social comparison,' which decreases happiness."[11] This article on "inciting envy" actually incited some outrage because many responded by saying it is not envy they feel but *anger*: anger at wealth and wage disparity; anger that such a small percentage of people control so much of the wealth; anger that the game seems rigged. Brooks sites a Pew survey that shows how envy is actually linked to lack of opportunity:

According to Pew, the percentage of Americans who feel that "most people who want to get ahead" can do so through hard work has dropped by 14 points since about 2000. As recently as 2007, Gallup found that 70 percent were satisfied with their opportunities to get ahead by working hard; only 29 percent were dissatisfied.

Today, that gap has shrunk to 54 percent satisfied, and 45 percent dissatisfied. In just a few years, we have gone from seeing our economy as a real meritocracy to viewing it as something closer to a coin flip.[12]

There is clear evidence that since the Great Recession of 2008–2009, there is growing frustration with wealth disparity and a perceived lack of opportunity for upward mobility in our country. Brooks concludes the article by saying, "We must recognize that fomenting bitterness over income differences may be powerful politics, but it injures our nation. We need aspirational leaders willing to do the hard work of uniting Americans around an optimistic vision in which anyone can earn his or her success. This will never happen when we vilify the rich or give up on the poor."[13]

Hauerwas and Willimon persistently argue that there is a close connection between greed and envy. Both are spiritual problems.

> Envy, the close cousin of greed, is infinitely more subtle. Envy loves to adorn itself as "service to others" through which we acquire power in order to "do some good." We climb to the top of the company ladder, not for ourselves, but in service to the advancement of women everywhere. We become the corporate attorney so that we can give a few hours a month to pro bono work. We say all we want is simply to be able to do what good we can do. Our want is the root of the problem. Desire. What we want is power and status.[14]

This poses an interesting question: What is the line between desiring power and status and simply desiring significance and affirmation? After all, we all want to feel as though our lives matter. We all want to feel valued and appreciated. Yet we continue to search for significance and security in all the wrong places. "Like the rich fool in Jesus' parable, we attempt to resist knowledge of our own insignificance by insulating ourselves with things. Alas, we find that no matter what we have acquired, there is always someone we envy."[15] Envy is the opposite of gratitude, and gratitude is a sign of Christian maturity. Preaching the importance of gratitude and thanksgiving is a way to address the issue of envy.

For pastors preaching to affluent congregations in North America, addressing the dangers of materialism, greed, and envy should be a priority. Every human being is guilty of coveting to some degree. According to Hauerwas and Willimon, "The commandment against covetousness may be one of the most accusatory for those of us who live in a society of seemingly unquenchable acquisitiveness, where greed appears to be a necessary component to keep the economy running smoothly."[16] After all, the United States of America was founded to give its citizens certain rights and freedoms—among those are life, liberty, and the pursuit of happiness. This "pursuit" is where things get complicated. "The Constitution tells us that America exists to give people what we want, without judging the comparative worth of our wants. To not want is almost un-American."[17] But, as Americans, our "wants" get us into trouble. Our wants only seem to increase. We have a difficult time differentiating between our "wants" and our "needs." And in a competitive culture, when somebody has something that we don't have, it is easy to find ourselves wanting it. For Hauerwas, this is the aspect of American culture that makes inner peace very challenging. And if there is to ever be peace in the world, it must begin with inner peace.

Hauerwas wrote a classic book in 1983 titled *The Peaceable Kingdom*. This work has been used as the primary text for many classes on Christian ethics at both the graduate and undergraduate levels. Throughout the book, Hauerwas articulates his belief that materialism and consumption often lead to a lack of inner peace. When Jesus calls his disciples, he asks them to leave everything behind and follow him. "They are to make a radical break with security and possessions, with the customs and habits of everyday life, for no other purpose than to share in his ministry of preaching the repentance needed to become part of the kingdom (Mark 3:13; Matt. 10:5)."[18] Of course, this begs the question, "What does it mean to follow Jesus today? What are we called to leave behind?" Many of us are disciples, but we don't leave everything behind to follow Christ. For us, the real questions are: "How attached are we to our possessions? Do they define us? Can we exist apart from them?" According to Hauerwas, "Discipleship is quite simply extended training in being dispossessed. To become followers of Jesus means that we must, like him, be dispossessed of all that we think gives us power over our own lives and the lives of others. Unless we learn to relinquish our presumption that we can ensure the significance of our lives, we are not capable of the peace of God's kingdom."[19] This helps explain why there are so many Christians who lack inner peace. Possessions can quickly become possessive. Yet many cannot imagine life without the "security" of material things. Hauerwas is asking where we find our meaning and security in life. Ultimately it must come from God and not from money and possessions.

But Hauerwas takes his case a step further in saying that possessions often lead to anger, fear, and even violence. "For our possessions are the source of our violence. Fearing that others desire what we have, or stung by the seldom acknowledged sense that what we have we do not deserve, we seek self-deceptive justifications that mire us in patterns of injustice which can be sustained only through coercion."[20] According to Hauerwas, human beings have always been very good at self-deception.

Identifying and confronting self-deception is never easy. In the Sermon on the Mount, Jesus asks, "Why do you see the speck in your neighbor's eye but do not notice the log in your own eye? Or how can you say to your neighbor, 'Let me take the speck out of your eye' while the log is in your own eye? You hypocrite, first, take the log out of your own eye, and then you will see clearly to take the speck in your neighbor's eye."[21] It is easy to recognize greed in others but not in ourselves. It seems that somebody else always has more than we do. Hauerwas says, "Of course we believe our most precious possession to be the self we have created, that we have chosen. Such a possession we do not lose—as we see clearly in the character of the disciples in the Gospels—simply by willing to give up all we have. What Jesus offers is a journey, an adventure. Once undertaken, we discover that what we once held valuable, even the self, we no longer count as anything."[22] The journey that Christ invites us on is a journey to get over ourselves, a journey to put others first. It's a journey to resist selfishness and greed in order to truly care for others. Preoccupation with self and status is what leads to greed.

Joy

Many in our culture continuously turn to money and material things in order to find a sense of happiness. But happiness is always short lived. It comes and goes. It does not last.

We often confuse happiness and joy, treating them as if they were same, but they are not. There is a significant difference between happiness and joy. Happiness is fleeting while joy is sustaining. Hauerwas makes a compelling case: "The irony is that the more we lose, the greater the possibility we have for living life joyfully. For joy is the disposition that comes from our readiness always to be surprised; or put even more strongly, joy is the disposition that comes from our realization that we can trust in surprises for the sustaining of our lives."[23]

Researchers such as Phillip Jenkins have shown that Christianity seems to be growing fastest in Third World countries. There God is not competing with money and possessions or with excessive materialism. Joy seems to be greater among those who have very little. Hauerwas says, "Perhaps the most remarkable aspect of learning to live joyfully is that we learn to see the simple and most common aspects of our existence, such as our friends, our spouses, our children, as sheer gifts to which we have no right but who are nonetheless present to us."[24] In affluent cultures, the more we have, the more we want. The more we make, the more we spend. If we are not careful, we can quickly lose sight of what matters the most. I have often said in sermons that we are guilty of "loving things and using people rather than loving people and using things."

For a number of years now, our church has sent mission teams to Swaziland, Africa. In Swaziland, wealth is not measured by money or possessions. The people have little to nothing. Wealth, then, is measured by relationships. Faith and joy are clearly evident among the Swazi people. Others who live in Third World countries do not have much either, but they are also not enslaved to much.

Consider the irony. A movement that started in Galilee among the peasant class has become the preferred religion of the wealthy and powerful in this country. And yet, we seem to be more possessed by our possessions than we are by Christ. Those of us in North America can learn a lot from those in Third World countries about dispossession and joy. We have so much, but we are often so miserable and we cannot seem to figure out why.

Fear and Control

Human beings long for control, and the more we possess, the more control we think we have and therefore the more control we want. For Hauerwas, "Our need to be in control is the basis for the violence of our lives. For since our 'control' and 'power' cannot help but be built on an insufficient basis, we must use force to maintain the illusion that we are in control. We are deeply afraid of losing what unity of self we have achieved. Any idea or person threatening that unity must be either manipulated or eliminated."[25] It seems true that as material possessions increase, so do fear and anxiety. Human beings are afraid of losing what they have and will do anything to protect it, even if it means resorting to violence. Conflict arises when we encounter others who we perceive as threats. "We fear others because they always stand as an implicit challenge to our deceptions. Thus it seems the inherent necessity of all people to have or create an enemy."[26] Addiction to money and material things is eerily similar to other addictions, such as alcohol, drugs, work, or sex. Enough is never enough. Through addiction we attempt to control our lives at all costs. The heart of the Serenity Prayer says this: "God grant me the serenity to accept the things I cannot change, the courage to change the things I can, and the wisdom to know the difference." Trying to control the uncontrollable does not lead to inner peace. Fear often drives materialism—fear of rejection, fear of not having enough, fear of not keeping up with everybody else. We are social beings, and societal pressures and expectations are strong and always present.

Fear is also related to insecurity and a lack of courage. Hauerwas and Willimon collaborated on a book together in 1989 titled *Resident Aliens: Life in the Christian Colony*. In that book they say: "We all know the way we rationalize and excuse our own covetousness, acquisitiveness, and greed. 'I'm not really that well off,' we say. 'I have all I can do to make ends meet.' 'I worked hard for this and I deserve it.' 'It's getting harder and harder to put food on the table.' Our lies are the correlate of our materialism, for both our materialism and our self-deceit are our attempts to deal with our insecurity, our finitude by taking matters into our own hands."[27] Again, we self-deceive often to convince others that greed and materialism are not issues in our lives. They are problems for other people, but not for us. "Luther called security the ultimate idol. And we have shown, time and again, our willingness to exchange anything—family, health, church, truth—for a taste of security. We are vulnerable animals who seek to secure and establish our lives in improper ways, living by our wits rather than faith."[28] It is certainly tempting to blame our tendency towards greed on our desire to survive. It's a tough, competitive world where everybody seems to be out for themselves. We fear not having enough. We fear running out of resources. We fear not being able to provide for our families. And, before we know it, we have turned ourselves into "God" and placed our hope in earthly things, which always disappoint.

The Church's Challenge in a Secular Age

When he came to guest lecture at Sewanee in the summer of 2013, I asked Stanley Hauerwas what he thought was the greatest challenge for Christians and the church in America today. He responded with one word: "idolatry." Idolatry manifests itself in many forms, with wealth and materialism being just one example. In chapter 1 of *The Truth About God*, when dealing with the first commandment, Hauerwas and Willimon state: "Idolatry is more than giving homage to finite realities, as destructive as that may be. Idolatry consists in the denial of the true God through failure to trust the only One who may be trusted. Idolatry is the assumption that salvation can come elsewhere than from the God who commands, *You shall have no other gods before me.*"[29] We live in an age when many view themselves as "self-made." They will say, "I came from nothing and look at all that I have done." Accomplishment and success often breed pride and arrogance. "The quest for autonomy (literally, self-law), for independence, self-sufficiency, to have ourselves as gods unto ourselves, is often seen as the hallmark of modernity. Faced with the apparent meaninglessness of a world without God, we assume that a major modern task is to create or impose meaning."[30] Charles Taylor, in his book *A Secular Age,* suggests that we now live in an age in which belief in God is no longer expected.[31] In the Introduction to his autobiographical memoir *Hannah's Child,* Hauerwas says, "Charles Taylor has characterized 'our age' as one of 'exclusive humanism.' God is a 'hypothesis' most people no longer need—and most people includes those who say that they believe in God. Indeed, when most people think it 'important' that they believe in God, you have an indication that the God they believe in cannot be the God who raised Jesus from the dead or Israel from Egypt."[32] As our age grows increasingly secular and faith in the one true God becomes less of a priority for many, idolatry will continue to manifest itself in a variety of forms.

Hauerwas and Willimon say that the first commandment of the Decalogue is what gives us meaning: "The Decalogue reminds us that the meaning of our lives is given through the discovery that we are indeed creatures of a gracious God who gives us all the time in the world to live in trust with one another. Meaning is a by-product of having been addressed by God in the first commandment."[33] Modernity, with all of its wealth, affluence, and illusions of self-sufficiency, has lured many away to a false sense of security. "Modern people like to think that as we become more educated, liberal, enlightened, the less we need to worship gods. No. We appear to have been created to worship and worship something we will."[34] Those with wealth and affluence tend to be most prone to turn away from God in order to find meaning and security in this world, which is idolatry. As in the case with the Rich Young Ruler, sometimes becoming dispossessed of possessions is the only way to see clearly again. Jesus said, "You cannot serve [both] God and wealth."[35]

For those preaching to affluent and wealthy congregations and for Christians who have been blessed financially in this world, the challenge is straightforward. Is it possible to be wealthy and to still serve and worship the one true God? I believe that the answer is yes, but Hauerwas warns that the dangers are real. The more we have, the more distracted we are. The more we have, the more controlling we are. The more we have, the more likely we are to believe in the fallacy of self-sufficiency. For Hauerwas and Willimon, it all comes back to the Eucharist and all that it represents:

> In the Eucharist we find the full reality of the Law, for there we discover that God has not abandoned us. In the Eucharist the law is given its *telos*, creating peace in a world that knows no peace. Our hungers are named, not as longing for the stuff of this world, but by a bit of bread and a sip of wine we learn to call just this much bread and this much wine a feast. It is all the more important therefore, for Christians to have our desires ordered by this great feast through which we learn God's love as truly unrelenting, seeking us all the way to the Cross.[36]

At the Table, we stand as equals before God, rich and poor, old and young, male and female, seeking to have our deepest desires met. And at the Table, they are met once and for all in the life, death, and resurrection of Jesus Christ.

Critiquing Hauerwas

I have tremendous respect for Stanley Hauerwas (and Will Willimon). His scholarship and writings have had a profound impact on my life and ministry. I admire his courage and audacity to speak out against idolatry and greed in our culture. He has recognized the need to speak to both the church and to the academy. He also understands that preaching is where the rubber meets the road, and he has become more inclined to preach himself in the later years of his career. I agree with much of what he says and writes. Although I do not agree with all of his perspectives, I find myself drawn to his critical thinking and honest approach. It is easy to see how he has changed the dialogue in Christian ethics and will be regarded for generations to come as a giant in his field.

Still, Hauerwas's views are open to honest criticism and disagreement. For example, Stephen Webb wrote an article in 2002 for *First Things* called "The Very American Stanley Hauerwas." In that article, he says:

Over the years I have become convinced that Hauerwas is right more often than he is wrong, but it is the way in which he is wrong that makes him so interesting. His hyperboles can let evangelicals off the hook from thinking about the critical issues liberal academics raise, and they can soothe the consciences of academics (like me) who are alienated from their liberal colleagues. Hyperbole is a seductive trope. It is so excessive that you can think you have done what it demands just by speaking it. But saying something does not make it so. Indeed, Hauerwas is so persuasive that his theology sounds too good to be true. That's because it is. Such rhetoric sounds good to those of us who believe that the Church has lost much of its integrity in the modern world.[37]

I find Webb's critique, analysis, and insights helpful in thinking about my own response to Hauerwas. There are three basic concerns that I have regarding Hauerwas's perspective on greed and materialism.

The first critique is simple and could even be considered petty: *Hauerwas has spent the majority of his career teaching at Duke University, a very expensive and elite private school.* For many years, he has personally benefitted from a system that could certainly be viewed as greedy. For parents to send a child to Duke without scholarship, the cost is over $60,000 per year, which includes room and board.[38] So, is it greedy or materialistic to save and spend this type of money for education purposes? Is that hoarding? Is that excessive? Is that necessary? Is that elitist? What would Jesus say about that amount of money being spent on a college or divinity education? Hauerwas and Willimon say, "Our problem as humans is not that we are full of desire, aflame with unfulfillment. Our problem is that we long for that which is unfulfilling."[39] Is it wrong to desire an education that could cost in excess of $250,000 in order to come sit in a classroom and be lectured on greed and materialism? There seems to be great irony in that proposition. Many say that the education bubble in our country will burst at some point. Time will tell. In the meantime, how are we to regard the exorbitant cost of attending Duke, and how does Hauerwas reconcile the cost of being at Duke given much of what he says?

Second, Hauerwas is correct to identify and critique national and economic idolatries, but his anti-American sentiment is repetitive and exhausting. In some ways, it is surprising that Hauerwas still wants to live in this country, especially given his ongoing frustration with the "American Way." Stephen Webb says:

> Perhaps the key to the reception of his work is his anti–Americanism. Hauerwas has given rise to a whole generation of theologians who make quick work of consumerism, patriotism, nationalism, and popular culture. Some of his students have told me that they are so alienated from American politics that they no longer vote. Nevertheless, his critique of all things American is what makes Hauerwas look more at home with liberals than conservatives. By continuously thumping on that theme, he is able to gain a larger academic audience than would ever listen to a more traditionally evangelical theologian. Indeed, without his constant critique of everything American, he would be in danger of looking like just another evangelical theologian.[40]

It would be nice to hear Hauerwas confirm some positive aspect of American culture in addition to constantly criticizing and degrading it. There must be some reason he has spent his entire career teaching and writing in this country and has not accepted a tenured chair overseas. It is true, many in our country are American or capitalistic before they are Christian, and he is correct in pointing that out. However, despite some of its flaws and missteps, we are still blessed to live in a wonderful country. America has done a lot of good, provided education and opportunity for millions, lifted many out of poverty, delivered humanitarian aid to millions, ended genocide in some countries, held dictators accountable, and much more.

In his book *Money, Greed, and God: Why Capitalism Is the Solution and Not the Problem*, Jay Richards of the Discovery Institute identifies what he sees as eight myths about capitalism. The first myth is called the "Nirvana Myth," or contrasting capitalism with an unrealizable ideal or utopia. He says, "When we ask whether we can build a just society, we need to keep the question nailed to solid ground: just compared with what? It doesn't do anyone any good to tear down a society that is unjust compared with the kingdom of God if that society is more just than any of the ones that will replace it. Compared with Nirvana, no real society looks good."[41] Capitalism is certainly not without its flaws, but it has fared much better than communism and socialism. Hauerwas would say that he does not have an economic policy, but he should not compare capitalism to some unrealizable ideal. This leads me to my final criticism.

Lastly, while not advocating for a particular economic policy or approach, Hauerwas walks a fine line in differentiating personal responsibility from greed. To repeat an earlier quote, he and Willimon write, "In the world in which we live, we have learned to call greed 'ambition' or 'providing for my family.' We have learned to call greed 'getting ahead.' We have learned to call greed 'working for a better life.' We have learned to call greed 'pleasure.'"[42] Greed is difficult to define because everybody has a different understanding of what it is. With these strong words, Hauerwas is equating ambition, providing for family, moving ahead, and upward mobility with greed. This may be part of his use of hyperbole to which Steven Webb refers, but these words may not be as prophetic as they are offensive. Life is difficult and expensive. Many struggle simply to survive. Just because people are trying to provide for their families does not mean that they are greedy. Who gets to define how much is enough? Does teaching at Duke constitute working for a better life? Is it greedy to send your child to Duke? Perhaps more than any other passage, these words demonstrate why greed is such a difficult and sensitive topic. Personal responsibility is a fundamental belief of many capitalists, and, like it or not, we live in a capitalistic culture. It seems as though Hauerwas might actually agree with Ayn Rand that capitalism is largely based on greed.

Jay Richards rejects that notion. He believes that greed is not the natural result of capitalism. He contends, "If you look, you can find greed all across the fruited plains and in every human heart. That's because we're fallen human beings, not because we are Americans. Every culture and walk of life has heaping helpings of greedy people. There are greedy doctors, greedy social workers, greedy teachers, politicians, park rangers, and youth pastors... [G]reed is universal, capitalism is not."[43] Hauerwas seems to imply that anybody who succeeds in the capitalist system and seeks to provide and take care of their family could be labeled greedy. That is simply not the case. It is one thing to say that capitalism may present the opportunity for greed to manifest itself, but it is wrong to imply that all people in a capitalistic system are greedy.

Hauerwas certainly gives preachers much to consider when preaching on the subject of money, materialism, and greed. It has always been easy for tenured academics to write and say whatever they like. But preachers who are in the pulpit Sunday after Sunday don't have that luxury or security. We must balance the prophetic with the pastoral when presenting the gospel to a materialistic culture. Jesus said, "Your life does not consist of the abundance of possessions," but how easily we tend to forget that. And that's not what the rest of society tells us. Preachers are called to challenge the materialistic culture, but to do it in a way that inspires rather than condemns.

Next I turn to a contemporary preacher in the mainline tradition who does an admirable job of balancing political diversity while addressing the issues of money and materialism.

CHAPTER 4

★ ★ ★ ★ ★ ★ ★ ★ ★ ★ ★ ★ ★ ★ ★

Adam Hamilton's Passion for the "Radical Center"

The Reverend Adam Hamilton grew up in the Kansas City area and earned a B.A. in pastoral ministry from Oral Roberts University. He went on to receive his Master of Divinity degree from the Perkins School of Theology at Southern Methodist University. In 1990, Hamilton founded the Church of the Resurrection in Leawood, Kansas. The original members met in a funeral home, which is how the church received its name. Over the past twenty-five years, the church has grown to become the largest United Methodist Church in North America, with over 20,000 members. It is considered by many to be the largest and most influential mainline church in the country today. Hamilton is a leader, visionary, author, and preacher. He is also a scholar.

One of the challenges in the church today, which is indicative of our society in general, is that the extreme positions are the most vocal. We have churches known for their liberal positions, and churches known for their conservative ones. What about those not comfortable with either extreme? What if the labels "liberal" and "conservative" are actually part of the problem? Hamilton tells the story about turning on the television one morning and seeing Jerry Falwell debate John Shelby Spong and then wondering to himself if those are the only two options that we have. Most mainline pastors are called to preach and minister to a diverse congregation—young and old, Republican and Democrat, rich and poor, liberal and conservative, often gay and straight. The question is how we do this effectively, realistically, and with integrity.

In his book *Seeing Gray in a World of Black and White*, Hamilton says:

> When people ask me, "Are you liberal or conservative?" my answer is usually, "Yes!" My answer is yes for several reasons. First, I see both liberals and conservatives as two parts of a whole. When we say that someone is liberal with their giving, we mean that he or she is generous. I want to be liberal in that sense of the word. If liberal is defined as "favoring reform," that, too, captures my heart as a Protestant, because it recalls one of the important Reformation slogans *ecclesia reformata, semper reformada:* "the church reformed, always reforming." If *liberal* is a synonym for "broad minded" or "open minded" then yes, I wish to be a liberal! Yet if "conservative" means holding on to what is good from the past, and being cautious in embracing change simply for the sake of change, then mark me conservative! If being conservative within the Christian community means retaining the historic doctrines of the Christian faith as articulated in the creeds, then I am conservative. If conservative means as the Latin, *conservare* does, guarding, keeping, or observing (presumably the treasures of the past), then at least with regards to many things, I must be conservative. On the other hand, if *liberal* means holding to the absolute right of individuals to do whatever they choose, or if *conservative* means simply seeking to maintain the status quo, I could not be defined as either liberal or conservative![1]

Passages like these have caused thousands of clergy and laity to resonate with Hamilton's message over the years. The truth is that there are many people who cannot be labeled as simply "liberal" or "conservative." Life is much more complex than that. "Even our most basic ways of seeing and categorizing people in our society—left/right, liberal/conservative—point us to the truth that the world is not always black and white, and more often than not, we find ourselves somewhere in the grey between the two."[2] Preachers are called to wrestle with this tension themselves and encourage parishioners to do the same.

For many years, Hamilton has been a leading advocate for a growing shift in Christianity to move toward what he calls the "radical center." In the last chapter of *Seeing Gray in a World of Black and White,* he says, "The radical center within the Christian faith embraces the evangelical gospel that proclaims that human beings are wounded by sin and are in need of saving, and that Jesus Christ is God's antidote to our human condition. And, it embraces the social gospel that seeks to love our neighbor as we love ourselves, and recognizes the Christian's responsibility for addressing the great problems of poverty, oppression, racism, the environment, and war."[3] Hamilton does not believe that it will make sense in the future to resort to the same old divisions within Christianity—right/left, liberal/ conservative. These divisions have been a major distraction for Christians "The evangelical gospel without the social gospel is spiritual narcissism. The social gospel without the evangelical gospel remains afflicted by sin and holds, in the words of the Apostle Paul, 'to the outward form of godliness but denying its power' (II Timothy 3:5a). The radical center holds that the gospel is incomplete without both its evangelical and social witness."[4] His message seems to be resonating today, and he is admired as a pioneer within the mainline church.

In the Introduction to his book *Confronting the Controversies,* a compilation of a sermon series he preached at Church of the Resurrection on controversial topics, Hamilton talks about his own background and how it has enabled him to maintain a balanced approach:

> I came to faith in Christ in a conservative church and in this church heard a call into ministry. My undergraduate degree in theology and pastoral care was from a conservative university. My seminary training, however, was firmly grounded in the more liberal

traditions of the United Methodist school of theology I attended. What I came to see in pursuing each of my degrees was that there are elements of truth on both sides of the great theological and sociological divide, but those on either side had a hard time hearing or respecting those on the other. This experience helped me appreciate and look for the truth in both sides of difficult issues. I have tried to practice the discipline of placing myself in the shoes of those on both sides of a debate who hold strong opinions. This leads to a key component of addressing controversial issues: People of opposite perspectives want to feel that their position has been heard, respected, and accurately represented. Individuals become hurt or frustrated when a trusted friend or teacher speaks to a complex issue and argues persuasively for one side while failing to represent the opposing view adequately. This is especially the case if one has not taken into account the deep motivations that guide people's opinions and convictions.[5]

Because of his exposure to diverse theological and social positions, Hamilton has been effective at reaching both because he understands both. This is a helpful insight into his success as a pastor and preacher. He has an unusual preaching style that affirms both positions before sharing what he believes.

Hamilton is very different from Hauerwas in that he is a pastor first and foremost, not simply an academic. Although he takes scholarship very seriously (even making the decision to recently move St. Paul's Seminary onto the campus of the Church of the Resurrection), Hamilton is not writing for an academic audience. He is writing to inspire laity and other clergy. He is concerned about the future of mainline Christianity, theological and social divisions in the church, labels, political polarization, and how we can be unified to address the important issues of our day. He realizes that marginalizing people because of their position or ideology will accomplish nothing. Whereas Hauerwas is not afraid to pick a fight, stand his ground, and even offend, Hamilton maintains a more pastoral and balanced approach to addressing the tough issues. He wants to bring people together for the common good. Both Hauerwas and Hamilton seem to empathize with evangelical convictions (Jesus resurrected) while maintaining a strong social conscience. Hamilton's tone is certainly less rigid than Hauerwas's. However, Hauerwas's work has been a source of inspiration for Hamilton over the years. Hamilton concludes *Seeing Gray* by reiterating something that he says in the Introduction:

> Christianity is in need of a new reformation. The Fundamentalism of the last century is waning. And the Liberalism of the last fifty years has jettisoned too much of the historic Christian gospel to take its place. Christianity's next reformation will strike a middle path between Jerry Falwell and John Shelby Spong. It will draw upon what is best in both Fundamentalism and Liberalism by holding together the evangelical and social gospels, by combining a love of Scripture with a willingness to see both its humanity as well as its divinity, and by coupling a passionate desire to follow Jesus Christ with a reclamation of his heart toward those whom religious people have often rejected. This reformation will be led by people who are able to see the gray in a world of black and white.[6]

Hamilton has exhibited his ability to find the radical center when dealing with a host of controversial issues, including evolution, hell, theodicy, abortion, war, the death penalty, euthanasia, homosexuality, the separation of church and state, and biblical interpretation. He believes that there must room in the church for multiple positions. Let us now look to see how he addresses the challenging subjects of money, materialism, and contentment.

American Dream or Nightmare?

Hamilton published a book in the spring of 2009 titled *Enough: Discovering Joy through Simplicity and Generosity.* His timing could not have been better since that was the period when the stock market reached its lowest point. The United

States was in the throes of what would later be called the "Great Recession," and there was widespread fear and panic in our nation. Banks were failing. Corporations were folding. Barack Obama had just assumed the office of president in January and had quite a mess to clean up. The economy was in a free fall, and many were fearing another Depression. The first chapter of Hamilton's book is titled "When Dreams Become Nightmares," and Hamilton quotes Alexis de Tocqueville, a political philosopher who came to America in the nineteenth century and made this observation:

> Americans are extremely eager in the pursuit of immediate material pleasures and are always discontented with the position that they occupy... They think about nothing but ways of changing their lot and bettering it. For people in this frame of mind every new way of getting wealth more quickly, every machine which lessens work, every means of diminishing the cost of production, every invention which makes pleasures easier or greater, seems the most magnificent accomplishment of the human mind... One usually finds that the love of money is either the chief or a secondary motive at the bottom of everything the Americans do. This gives a family likeness to all their passions and soon makes them wearisome to contemplate.[7]

The American Dream has been defined in many different ways. Some say it is simply the opportunity for upward mobility. Others say it is allowing each generation to do better than the one before it. Some say it is the ability to accumulate wealth, which then leads to opportunity. Others describe it as a house with a white picket fence, two cars, and two children. Whatever the definition of the American Dream, many would acquiesce that purchasing power and acquisition of material goods are part of it. Hamilton says, "The love of money and the things money can buy is indeed a primary or secondary motive behind most of what we do. Consuming, acquiring, buying—this is what the American Dream has come to mean."[8] However, Hamilton makes it clear that in 2008–2009, the American Dream quickly evolved into the American Nightmare.

He refers to two basic problems that led to the Great Recession: *affluenza* and *credit-itis*. *Affluenza* can be defined as: "1 The bloated, sluggish, and unfulfilled feeling that results from efforts to keep up with the Joneses. 2 An epidemic of stress, overwork, waste, and indebtedness caused by dogged pursuit of the American Dream. 3 An unsustainable addiction to economic growth."[9] Many, including de Tocqueville, have observed how many believe that one is not truly American unless affected by this addiction. We often go shopping, not because we need anything, but because that is something to do. Then, once at the mall or store, we find something that we simply "must" have and cannot live without. And because the things that we buy only satisfy us for a short while, we are back at it before we know it. Hamilton says, "No doubt you can quickly think of something you hope to purchase next—new clothes, new computer, new furniture, a new car, a new kitchen, a new home. We all need the continued feeling of our desire for more. And yet we do not have room for all the stuff that we already have."[10]

The second factor that turned the American Dream into the American Nightmare is what Hamilton calls *credit-itis*. Simply defined, *credit-itis* is "the opportunity for us to buy now and pay later." He adds, "It's basically the idea that you can enjoy something today and pay for it tomorrow, and it feeds on our desire for instant gratification. Our economy today is built on the concept of credit-itis. Unfortunately, it has exploited our lack of self-discipline and allowed us to feed our affluenza, wreaking havoc in our personal and national finances."[11]

Both affluenza and credi-itis are addicting, and many people do not realize that they are in trouble until it is too late. This leads to some important questions: Why do so many Americans believe we can spend money that we do not have? Why are we unable to live within our means and appreciate what we already have? What created this culture of constant consumption, and how can we get it under control? How can we begin to understand that life is about more than what we an buy?

For Hamilton, the problem is clearly spiritual. The American Nightmare was the result of a spiritual void in our culture that we are seeking to fill with consumption and materialism. As he puts it:

Inside us there is a brokenness; the Bible calls it sin. Our souls were created in the image of God, but they have been distorted. We were meant to desire God, but we have turned that desire toward possessions. We were meant to find our security in God, but we find it in amassing wealth. We were meant to love people but instead we compete with them. We were meant to enjoy the simple pleasures of life, but we busy ourselves with pursuing money and things. We were meant to be generous and to share with those in need, but we selfishly hoard our resources for ourselves. There is a sin nature within us. Three of the seven deadly sins relate directly to the problem we have with money and possessions. First, we are afflicted by *envy* or covetousness. We want what others have and we will do anything we can do get it—whether that means taking it or buying it for ourselves. Second, we are afflicted by *greed* or avarice. We have an intense desire for more and don't want to share what we have. And third, we are afflicted with *gluttony*. We keep consuming even when we are full and our needs are met—and we finally make ourselves sick.[12]

This analysis is reminiscent of Hauerwas's and Willimon's words regarding greed, envy, and idolatry in *The Truth About God*. Hamilton would agree that we continue to seek security and meaning in the wrong things. We continue to look to what others have and then convince ourselves that we want and need it. When life becomes all about competition and consumption, something has gone astray.

For Hamilton, spiritual freedom can be found in simplicity and restraint. He is not advocating a world where consumption does not happen but where it is held in check. He is advocating a world where we learn to live within our means and be thankful for what we have. He says, "I am suggesting that, with the help of God, we aim to simplify our lives and silence the voices constantly telling us we need more; that we live counter culturally by actually living below, not above, our means; that we build in what we need to be able to live generously and faithfully. And in doing so, we will discover the many gifts of simplicity."[13] In John's Gospel, Jesus says, "I came that they may have life, and have it abundantly."[14] Hamilton makes the case that we simply cannot enjoy fullness of life if we are constantly trying to keep up with the Joneses and acquire what we do not already have. Learning to simplify can be very healthy.

Confronting Restlessness and Finding Contentment

Restlessness is a spiritual problem in any affluent culture. Those who are used to getting what they want when they want it seem to constantly want more. Discontentment is a major obstacle to growing spiritually, and restlessness is how it manifests itself. On the other hand, states Hamilton, we also have an inclination to be content with the wrong things: "God wants us to be content with certain things and discontent with other things. The problem is that we tend to get them confused. We tend to be discontent with those things we are supposed to be content with and content with those things we are supposed to be discontent with."[15] He refers to the great Scottish philosopher and politician James Mackintosh, who once said, "It is right to be content with what we have but never with what we are." Hamilton then says:

> It is a positive motivator to be discontent with our moral character, our spiritual life, our pursuit of holiness, our desire for justice, and our ability to love. These are areas in which we should continue to grow and improve, for we are meant to become more than we are today. We are meant to know God more, to cultivate a deeper prayer life, to pursue justice and holiness with increasing fervor, to love others more, and to grow in grace and character and wisdom with every passing day. The problem is that we tend to be content with our involvement in pursuing justice in the world. We tend to be content with our level of righteousness–sometimes being self-righteous. We tend to be content with how much we love others. We tend to be content with our relationship with God. We tend to be content with how often we read the Bible and pray. Generally we are satisfied with those things that

deserve more of our time and attention. Likewise, those things we should be content with are the very things we find ourselves hopelessly discontented with. Most of us experience discontentment with our stuff—our homes, cars, televisions, gadgets, clothes, and a whole host of other things.[16]

Hamilton points out that the goal is not to be content with everything but to be content with the right things. This is one of the greatest challenges in a competitive, capitalistic culture. Simply put, how do we find spiritual contentment in a competitive culture that is built upon and obsessed with more? This is a profound spiritual challenge that effective preaching must address.

Like any good preacher, Hamilton gets biblical, specific, and practical when dealing with the topic of contentment. Effective preaching cannot be just academic or theoretical. It must be practical and applicable. Hamilton grounds his advice in the powerful words of the apostle Paul, who writes to the Philippians: "I have learned to be content with whatever I have. I know what it is to have little, and I know what it is to have plenty. In any and all circumstances I have learned the secret of being well-fed and of going hungry, of having plenty and of being in need."[17] These words have even greater meaning when we remember that Paul wrote them from a prison cell in Rome, wondering if his life would be spared.

Building on Paul, Hamilton offers four keys to cultivating contentment in life. The first is to "remember that it could be worse." He attributes the phrase to John Ortberg, but says, "It is recognizing that no matter what we may like about a thing or person or circumstance, we can always find something good to focus on if only we will choose to do so."[18] The problem with many in our culture today is that we are so preoccupied with what is wrong that we fail to see the good. Earlier in his epistle to the Philippians, Paul writes, "Whatever is true, whatever is honorable, whatever is just, whatever is pure,... whatever is commendable, if there is any excellence and if there is anything worthy of praise, think about these things."[19] Like Paul, Hamilton is aware that we are able choose our attitude in life and what our focus will be. If we only look for what is wrong, we will find it. But if we look for that which is good, it is there. Things can always be worse.

Second, Hamilton says that, in order to cultivate contentment, we should ask ourselves, "How long will this make me happy?" It's a question that we often fail to ask in advance of a particular purchase because we are caught up in the moment and in our desire to own whatever it is that we want. "So often we buy something, thinking it will make us happy, only to find that the happiness lasts about as long as it takes to open the box. There is a brief moment of satisfaction when we make the purchase, but the item does not continue to bring satisfaction over a period of time. Many of the things we buy simply are not worth the expense."[20] The expectation that material goods will fill a spiritual void has always been wrong. As Hauerwas says, true discipleship involves learning what it means to become "dispossessed." Hauerwas and Hamilton would agree that joy is found in giving (and in losing) much more so than in consuming. Joy and happiness are different. Happiness is fleeting. Joy is sustaining. Many people in our culture continue to confuse the two.

Third, Hamilton says that to cultivate contentment we need to "develop a grateful heart." Again he draws on the words of Paul, who writes to the Thessalonians to "give thanks in all circumstances."[21] Gratitude is a skill that must be intentionally developed. Hamilton says, "Contentment comes when we spend more time giving thanks for what we have than thinking about what's missing or wrong in our lives. In any situation, we can either complain or be grateful. We can focus on all the things we don't like, or we can begin to search for the things we do like and be grateful for them. We can focus on the disappointments, or we can give thanks for the blessings."[22] Hamilton is aware that in a capitalistic culture it seems as though we are trained to constantly want more while continuing to find ourselves dissatisfied. This is the opposite of gratitude. Harvard psychiatrist Armand Nicholi Jr. wrote an essay called "Hope in a Secular Age," in which he stated: "What often appears to be the cause of despondency in many today is an awareness of a gap between what they think they ought to be and what they feel that they are. That is, there is a discrepancy between an ideal that they hold for themselves and at times think they measure up to, and an acute awareness of how far short they fall from the ideal."[23] Developing a grateful heart will always be a challenge in a culture in which marketers only want you to think about what you do not yet have. Despair can come when we compare ourselves to others. Gratitude comes when we thank God for what we have.

Lastly, Hamilton says that to cultivate contentment in our lives, we should ask ourselves, "Where does my soul find true satisfaction?" "This is why Augustine's words, written more than 1,600 years ago, still ring true today: 'Thou hast made us for thyself, O Lord, and our hearts are restless until they find their rest in thee.'"[24] For both Augustine and Hamilton, true contentment comes from God. Hamilton writes: "Deep in our hearts, we too desire to be connected with the one who is the Creator of the universe. We need to believe our lives have meaning. We need to know there is grace and mercy when we have blown it. We need to know there is hope in the face of the darkest circumstances. We need to know we are loved unconditionally by Someone who knows us better than we know ourselves. And we need to be able to share this love in meaningful relationships with others."[25] When all is said and done, Hamilton is convinced that contentment only comes through relationships—a relationship with God first, and then with others.

Restlessness is the inevitable result of trying to find contentment through the ongoing consumption of material goods. This is a profound truth that must be understood and then experienced. There are multiple ways that human beings deal with restlessness—alcohol, drugs, sex, work, consumption of goods, etc.—but at the end of the day, restlessness in life is a spiritual problem, a deep longing for God. Materialism is simply a symptom of a much deeper hunger. It has always been much easier to go to the mall than to wrestle with the deeper and more profound questions of meaning.

From Fear to Generosity

Hauerwas and Hamilton agree that fear is the driving force behind much of our human behavior. We fear not having enough. We fear a lack of security. We fear rejection and a lack of approval from friends. We fear not being able to keep up with everybody else. Fear is not always a negative thing; it often aids in survival. But fear is clearly a powerful force. At the end of *Enough*, Hamilton addresses the issue of fear: "Fear is a part of the defense mechanism God has built into each of us. The brain produces a series of responses to a perceived threat, and we adapt to the threat by either fleeing from it, preparing to fight, or finding other ways to protect ourselves."[26] Accumulating money and material goods is common response to fear.

The Great Recession of 2008 took levels of fear to new heights. It created widespread fear and panic, and many individuals have been slow to let those emotions go. Hamilton says, "If we're not careful, fear will beget fear and, at some point, the fear will outpace the reality. This is when our fear begins to shape the reality, becoming a self-fulfilling prophecy, and we find ourselves incapacitated by it. More than that, living in fear means not really living at all. If we give in to all of our fears, we will never do anything worth doing. And we will have missed out on opportunity and joy."[27] Again, Hamilton and Hauerwas agree that joy is a hallmark of the Christian life, but is incredibly difficult to experience when overcome by fear.

Hamilton is convinced that one of the most effective ways to overcome fear is through generosity, to move beyond self and to begin living a life for others. Excessive materialism is often a sign of somebody all wrapped up in themselves. When Christ becomes alive in our hearts, there is a dramatic shift that takes place. Hamilton offers a theological rationale for this shift, based on the words of Christ:

> As the Holy Spirit continues to work in our lives, we begin to think less about ourselves and more about others. We begin to see the needs of others and wonder, If I don't do something, who will? As this change takes place within us, we experience real joy. We discover that we find more joy in doing things for other people and for God than we ever did in doing things for ourselves. This is what Jesus meant when he said, "It is more blessed to give than to receive" (Acts 20:35). In the very act of losing our lives, we find life, just as Jesus

said, "For those who want to save their life will lose it, and those who lose their life for my sake will find it" (Matthew 16:25).[28]

Jesus was certainly aware that selfishness will keep us from spiritual growth, and so he calls us to move beyond self.

We now live in an age that is becoming more and more individualized and isolated through new forms of technology. Marketers now cater to the slogan "You deserve this!" Narcissism is on the rise. Yet, at the same time, depression has reached new heights. Preachers must effectively make the case that generosity not only helps others but fundamentally changes us as well. Hamilton observes, "Our generosity to God and others not only touches God and other people, it also changes us. As human beings, we were created with the need to be generous. When we are not generous in giving of what we have, we have not only a financial problem but also a spiritual problem."[29] Self-absorption and spiritual growth do not complement each other. Yet in an age when many say they are "spiritual but not religious," how many actually make the connection between spiritual growth and generosity? Hamilton states, "Generosity changes us, filling us with joy and filling our lives with blessings. When we are generous with what we have, we find that unexpected blessings flow back into our lives, catching us by surprise."[30] Hauerwas would agree. After all, in *The Peaceable Kingdom,* he says, "Joy is the disposition that comes from our readiness always to be surprised; or put even more strongly, joy is the disposition that comes from our realization that we can trust in surprises for the sustaining of our lives."[31] For Hamilton, true generosity is the secret to joy.

Hamilton points out that there are obvious reasons why many fail to be generous, the primary being the fear that there will not be enough left over. Therefore, generosity is an act of faith. Generosity is a spiritual discipline, one of Paul's "fruits of the spirit" found in Galatians 5:22. Hamilton says, "The more we grow in Christ, the more generous we become, because generosity is a fruit of spiritual growth. Our giving—both to God and to others—is actually a measure of spiritual growth, because giving requires that we trust God to supply our needs."[32] Faithful Christian stewardship must begin with an acknowledgment that everything we have, even life itself, is a gift from God. Even our ability to work, earn a profit, and create wealth is a gift from God. This should put to rest once and for all the myth of the self-made person. God gives us life, and we are merely stewards of all that we have. Fear will always leave us wondering if there will be enough. Faith is the assurance that God will provide. Therefore generosity and faith go hand in hand. They are the best combination for overcoming our fear of not having enough.

Tithing is a practical way that Christians practice generosity. The concept of tithing is firmly grounded in scripture (Lev. 27:30; Mal. 3:10). Hamilton points out that tithing, giving ten percent of our income for God's purposes, may seem overwhelming at first, but it is something that we can all grow into. Christians should make it a goal to move in the direction of tithing. Hamilton encourages his congregation to take incremental steps toward this end. "Perhaps you can give 2 percent or 5 percent or 7 percent. God understands where you are, and God will help you make the adjustments necessary for you to become more and more generous."[33]

Many preachers are afraid to preach tithing. This typically happens for two reasons. First, they may not be tithers themselves and therefore it is hypocritical to ask others to tithe. Second, for somebody giving minimally to the church, tithing may seem like an overwhelming goal and impossible to achieve. Hamilton, however, believes it is a spiritual goal to move toward the tithe. Tithing is a way that we confront fear and put our faith in God in action, trusting that all of our needs will be met.

Sermon for a President

In January of 2013, Adam Hamilton was invited to deliver the sermon at the National Prayer Service in Washington's National Cathedral as part of President Barack Obama's second Inauguration. This invitation demonstrated that Hamilton has become one of the most highly respected and effective preachers in the country. Based on the story of Moses, this sermon gives insight into Hamilton's homiletical style, his passion, and his priorities as a pastor. He first focuses on Moses' humility and compassion for the poor and how that should be an example for any type of religious or political leader:

> I begin first with the heart and character of Moses. There are two things we learn about Moses' heart and character in the Scriptures. Numbers tells us that the man Moses was a humble man, more humble than anyone else on the face of the earth. God chooses and uses those who humble themselves before him and before others. Young Mary, the mother of Jesus in her Magnificent says that God "scatters the proud and the thoughts of their hearts but lifts up the lowly." Jesus teaches the same thing. While his disciples were arguing over who was the greatest, Jesus says, "You don't understand, that's how the kings of the world operate but that's not how you operate." He said, "The first among you, the one who would be great, will be your servant." Then he washed his disciples' feet.
>
> Now, Moses' humility was coupled with a deep compassion and concern for the marginalized and the oppressed. He was raised in Pharaoh's palace, he had everything a man could possibly want, but when he saw the plight of the Hebrew slaves, he could not remain in silence and he could not remain in the palace. Ultimately, he risked his life to stand before Pharaoh and to demand that Pharaoh release the slaves. And he led them into the wilderness towards the Promised Land.
>
> This is what God looks for in the Scriptures from every king, every rabbi, every leader. He looks for those who will take seriously the call to justice, to do kindness, to speak up for those who cannot speak up for themselves. James says it this way, "True religion and undefiled before God is to care for the widows and the orphans." For Jesus at the Last Judgment it all comes down to this—"How did you respond to the needs of the least of these?" This is America at her best. At our best, we're a humble people. And we remember the call to have compassion for the least of these.[34]

Second, Hamilton focuses on Moses' ability to lead and his vision for the Israeli people in the face of great adversity:

Professor John Kotter, now retired from Harvard Business School, noted that two of the most important tasks of any leader are to cast a compelling vision for the future and then to motivate and inspire people to pursue it. That vision has to be a clear and compelling picture of where we want to go, our preferred picture of the future. Moses led the slaves out of Egypt, but that was not enough. Very quickly they grumbled and began to go back to Egypt where there were leeks and cucumbers to eat. It was at least safe there; the wilderness was hard. Moses had to constantly remind them of the vision. He said, "We're marching to the promised land, a land flowing with milk and honey, where we can worship freely, where we can love, where we can practice justice, where we can live in harmony."

A compelling vision unifies us. It excites us, it leads people to a willingness to sacrifice, and imbues them with a sense of purpose. Kotter suggested that the average American company struggled with a lack of vision, a compelling vision at least. As a pastor, I can tell you the same is true of local churches. [There are] congregations across the country that don't remember their purpose, and they no longer see a compelling vision for the future. And sadly this feels true of America today. With our two-party system, vision-casting often feels like mere political rhetoric. And we typically are offered two different visions, competing with one another, not one unifying vision.

To many Americans, we feel like a house divided that cannot stand. We find ourselves desperately longing to find common ground. To find a common vision, to be one nation, indivisible with liberty and justice for everyone. In this city, and in this room, are the people who can help. This may be, this bringing together of our country, a more important issue than anything else we face: because until we resolve our issues here or at least find some unifying vision that brings us together, we're going to find it very, very difficult to solve any other problems we're facing—debt ceilings, issues of healthcare.

Proverbs notes this: without a vision, the people perish. They don't literally perish. They just bicker and fight and become so polarized they can't get anything done.

We're in need of a new common national vision. Not one that is solely Democratic or solely Republican. We need one or two goals or dreams that Americans on both sides of the aisle can come together [on] and say, "Yes, that's what it means to be American." That's where we need to go.[35]

Hamilton acknowledges that we have a divided country. Partisan bickering and positioning keeps many things from getting done. But he uses his own congregation as an example of what can happen when people with different ideologies come together. The Church of the Resurrection in Kansas City has helped the poor and marginalized in their community:

For one small example of the power of vision [I will take an example] from the church that I serve in Kansas City—One of our visions at the church is to address the root causes of poverty in Kansas City so that our city might look more like the kingdom of God that Jesus preached about. And when we began to ask, "How do you address the root causes of poverty?" what we learned [is] that [one thing] everyone agrees upon is early childhood education. And so we had a vision that we would work, together with the public schools in Kansas City, to find a way to give the 2,284 children in six elementary schools where 90% of those children are on the free or reduced lunch program a chance for a better future. We partnered with these schools; we came and we said, "We don't have the answers, we just offer ourselves as servants. What do you need? How can we help?"

This last year, 2,500 of our members volunteered at those schools. We built playgrounds at all six of those schools where they didn't have playgrounds before. We repainted the insides of the schools where they didn't have money to fix the schools. Our members volunteered as tutors to read to the children. We purchased 20,000 books and gave them to the children so that they might read at home. When we found out that 1,400 children were coming to school hungry on Monday, because they didn't have the reduced lunch program at home over the weekend, we started providing backpacks for children with nutritious snacks every Friday, 1,400 of them, that our members pack and then deliver, so the children come back to school Monday fed. When we learned that 300 children sleep on the floor at home or on the couch in their homes, we provided 300 beds. We delivered them, we provided sheets and blankets and pajamas for these children.

On Christmas Eve, the biggest night of the year at our church, we voted a number of years ago to give away the entire Christmas Eve offering to projects benefiting children and poverty. And we challenged our members—Would you consider giving an amount equal to what you spend on your own children at Christmas in this offering? We give half of it to the projects benefiting a thousand orphans in Malawi, and half of it to the projects benefiting the 2,284 children in Kansas City. And on Christmas Eve, our folks in one evening gave $1.235 million to these projects.

I mention that not to brag, though I'm very proud of our congregation. But to say that's one congregation with one vision and that unifies us as a church. We're Democrats and Republicans in our congregation, we're left and right, conservative and liberal, but somehow these kinds of visions pull us together into the future. They excite and they help change the world.[36]

For Hamilton, compassion is lived out through ministry, collaboration, and generosity. He is convinced that leaders can inspire entire communities to be transformed when the love of Christ takes hold, a vision is set, and church is on fire.

Lastly, he concludes the Inaugural Sermon by showing the difficulties and challenges of leadership. Like Moses, courageous leaders have always and will always face criticism and opposition. No doubt, these words resonated with the President and the other elected leaders of our government attending the service:

> The last word I'd mention regarding Moses is, despite great opposition to his leadership, and despite feeling discouraged many times, he never gave up. To be a leader is to invite criticism. If you're a Sunday School teacher, they'll criticize you. If you're a supervisor at McDonald's, they'll criticize you. If you're a preacher, they'll criticize you...

> It was not long after Moses began to lead the children of Israel out of Egypt that they began to grumble against his leadership. Four years in, they disliked his policies so much, a number tried to vote him out of office. It was a close vote but somehow he managed to keep his job. In Numbers 11, we read that he went out into the wilderness—it's a wonderful and endearing story of Moses—and he lifts up his hands and he prays, "God, just kill me now. I don't want to do this anymore. It is too hard." But this was one time that God didn't answer Moses' prayer. Instead [God] said, in essence, "Get back to work. I need you."

> I'm reminded of the night in late January 1957 when Dr. Martin Luther King received a threatening phone call. His children and his wife were asleep. This wasn't his first threatening phone call. Since the Montgomery boycott, there had been many. But on this night, as his children and wife lay sleeping—he felt he couldn't go on. He began to think of a way, gracefully, to bow out of leadership of the movement. At midnight, he

bowed over the kitchen table, and he began to pray, "I'm afraid, Lord. The people are looking to me for leadership; if I stand before them without strength and courage, they, too, will falter. I'm at the end of my powers, God. I have nothing left. I've come to the point where I can't face it alone." And then he describes something interesting that happened next. He said, "I experienced the presence of the divine as I had never experienced God before. It seemed as though I could hear the quiet assurance of an inner voice saying, "Stand up for righteousness. Stand up for truth. And God will be at your side forever."

Imagine how the world would be different today if Dr. King had bowed out of leadership because it got just too hard—had he not stopped to pray that night, to seek God and God's reassurance?[37]

Although this sermon is certainly the most famous Hamilton has ever delivered to an international audience, it demonstrates who he is and his priorities as a pastor. He believes in the importance of humility and compassion. He believes that we are called to serve the poor and marginalized. He believes that leaders should set a vision and then inspire others to help achieve that vision. He believes that adversity is a part of life and leadership. He believes it is possible for a congregation to transform a community, and the Church of the Resurrection is an example of how that can happen. And he believes that all leaders must overcome criticism and adversity to achieve their goals. Hamilton continues to be an example of a mainline pastor who is able to address hot topics and politically divisive issues, including issues of wealth and materialism, in a constructive way that maintains the prophetic and pastoral balanced in a diverse congregation.

CHAPTER 5

★ ★ ★ ★ ★ ★ ★ ★ ★ ★ ★ ★ ★ ★

Preaching in a Materialistic Culture

In the introduction to his theological memoir *The Pastor,* Eugene Peterson profoundly observes: "I love being an American. I love this place in which I have been placed—its language, its history, its energy. But I don't love 'the American way,' its culture and values. I don't love the rampant consumerism that treats God as a product to be marketed. I don't love the dehumanizing ways that turn men, women, and children into impersonal roles and causes and statistics. I don't love the competitive spirit that treats others as rivals and even as enemies."[1] Peterson has identified the great contextual challenge for many North American preachers and pastors. We live in a materialistic culture in which everything seems to be measured by money; the almighty dollar has become a false god. The American way of life—with its emphasis on consumerism, materialism, and accumulation—has created a great challenge for those who seek to follow Jesus of Nazareth. Peterson says, "The cultural conditions in which I am immersed require, at least for me, a kind of fierce vigilance to guard my vocation from these cultural pollutants so dangerously toxic to persons who want to follow Jesus in the way that he is Jesus."[2] Jesus was an artisan and resonated with the peasant class. He lived a simple life. He showed compassion for the poor and challenged both the poor and the rich. He still does that today.

Both Stanley Hauerwas and Adam Hamilton wrestle with Jesus' teachings. One of the primary differences between

Hauerwas and Hamilton is that Hamilton must maintain a prophetic and pastoral balance in his congregation. Hauerwas does not have a congregation. In the world of academia, it seems that the more radical or sensational the statement or publication, the better. Preachers, on the other hand, who seek to deal realistically with hot political topics, must do so carefully and responsibly, remembering their pastoral responsibilities. This is a challenge that must be taken seriously. As stated earlier, Hamilton says, "Individuals become hurt or frustrated when a trusted friend or teacher speaks to complex issues and argues persuasively for one side while failing to represent the opposing view adequately. This is especially the case if one has not taken into account the deep motivations that guide people's opinions and convictions."[3] Hamilton's claim is true, including when dealing with the issues of money, possessions, and lifestyle. Money and Christian stewardship is a personal topic that makes many uncomfortable.

Over the years, the church has gained a reputation of always asking for money. Simply put, the church needs money to function, and faithful stewardship is part of the Christian life. Diminishing resources is an ongoing reality for many faith communities. However, at the heart of the conversation on money and stewardship is something much more important than the church's need to raise a budget. It is much more important than the offering plate and the building fund. The conversation about money and possessions is ultimately a conversation about priorities. Jesus said it best: "Where your treasure is, there your heart will be also."[4] Heart always follows treasure. Treasure does not always follow heart. This is a timeless truth for Christians. We communicate our values in life by deciding where to place our resources.

Guidance for the Road Ahead

Given our cultural situation, especially the grip that materialism has on America today, we preachers and laity who wish to preach and teach on the issue of money and materialism need guidance on how to do this. Below you will find ten observations I offer to you that have assisted me, and I trust will be beneficial to you as well.

1) ***Money is a universal reality in life that for many people has replaced God.*** Money is a necessity in the United States. It takes money to buy a house, pay rent, pay bills, buy groceries and clothes, raise and educate children, operate a church, and so on. Money, in and of itself, is not bad. What we do with it is what matters. How we spend money is the primary indicator of our values. Jesus knew that our heart follows our treasure, regardless of our race, nationality, age, sex, gender, class, sexual orientation, and other divisions. What we do with our money indicates how we value our money. In the nineteenth century, Frederick Nietzsche predicted that Western culture would soon replace God with money: "What was once done 'for the love of God' is now done for the love of money, i.e., for the love of that which at present affords us the highest feeling of power and a good conscience."[5] Sadly, his prediction has proven true for many in our culture. Presbyterian minister Tim Keller says, "Money is one of the most common counterfeit gods there is. When it takes hold of your heart it blinds you to what is happening, it controls you through your anxieties and lusts, and it brings you to put it ahead of all other things."[6] Money makes people do and say things they would not otherwise do and say. Andrew Carnegie said, "Man must have an idol—the amassing of wealth is one of the worst species of idolatry. No idol is more debasing than the worship of money."[7] Carnegie resigned from his business career early for this very reason, and wanted to use what he had to help others. The first commandment of the Decalogue is clear: "You shall have no other Gods before me," and Moses found the Israelites worshiping a golden calf upon returning from Sinai. The love of money fueled by materialism may be the greatest single threat to Christianity in North America because it often replaces God. This is a clear challenge to the spiritual life of many.

2) ***Preachers must make it abundantly clear how many times in scripture Jesus talks about money and possessions.*** There are roughly forty recorded parables

of Jesus in the gospels, and half of those deal directly with money. Examples include the parable of the rich fool (Lk. 12), the parable of the dishonest manager (Lk. 16), the parable of the rich ruler (Lk. 18), the parable of the laborers in the vineyard (Mt. 20), and many others. The Sermon on the Mount alone makes clear how serious Jesus was about this subject. "Do not store up for yourselves treasures on earth, where moth and rust consume and where thieves break in and steal; but store up for yourselves treasures in heaven, where neither moth nor rust consumes and where thieves do not break in and steal. For where your treasure is, there your heart will be also... No one can serve two masters; for a slave will either hate the one and love the other, or be devoted to the one and despise the other. You cannot serve God and wealth."[8] Preachers who avoid money passages in the gospels are not giving a thorough representation of Jesus' teaching. Certain pastors are guilty of only talking about money when the church needs money or is in the midst of a stewardship campaign. Mission and vision are also important during those times. Based on Jesus' teaching and the insights of scholars such as Hauerwas and Hamilton, I would recommend that money be talked about throughout the year, not just when the church is looking to raise a budget. Preachers who only talk about money during stewardship campaigns are guilty of using scriptures selectively for self-serving purposes. Money and materialism is a topic relevant to all and at all times. This simple fact cannot be ignored: Jesus talked about the subject often. Christians must wrestle with these texts despite the fact that they make us uncomfortable.

3) ***Greed is not defined by what we have but by whether or not we keep all we have to ourselves.*** Greed is a spiritual condition that crosses all socio-economic levels. Simply being "rich" does not make a person greedy. Being rich and never giving back makes a person greedy. Hauerwas and Willimon claim: "We

have learned to call greed 'ambition' or 'providing for my family.' We have learned to call greed 'getting ahead.' We have learned to call greed 'working for a better life.'"[9] However, I have argued that ambition, providing for family, and working for a better life are not the same things as greed. Many are working hard day after day to provide for their families and can hardly pay the bills, barely getting by. There are many others who have more than enough and feel as though they are strapped. Because money issues are private, we generally don't know what others make, when they are struggling, or if they are generous. Therefore, we can only determine for ourselves whether or not we are being greedy.

Hauerwas and Willimon also claim, "The good thing about greed is that unlike some sin, it is not subtle. Its results are public, there for all to see. Accumulation tends towards conspicuous display. If we cannot show others what we have accumulated, what's the good of accumulation?"[10] But I maintain that this is certainly not a universal truth. Indeed, there are some who have plenty and like to show it off. There are also some who pretend that they have plenty but are actually drowning in debt. Since money and possessions are the default scoreboard in our culture for determining whether or not a person is successful, Americans tend to judge by these measures. However, "conspicuous display" is not always evident. There are some who have a lot, who give a lot away, and who still have more than enough left over. This does not make them greedy. There are often hostility and resentment in our culture toward those who have means, and, in many cases, they are certainly unwarranted. There is nothing wrong with reaping the benefits of hard work as long as one remains generous and spiritually grounded in the process. Generosity is not defined by giving the bare minimum. No one socio-economic class has a monopoly on greed, because greed is a condition of the heart.

4) **Adam Hamilton is correct in his assertion that growing materialism is a clear indication of a much deeper spiritual void.** In *Enough*, Hamilton says, "We were meant to desire God, but we have turned that desire toward possessions. We were meant to find our security in God, but we find it in amassing wealth. We were meant to love people but instead we compete with them. We were meant to enjoy the simple pleasures of life, but we busy ourselves with pursuing money and things. We were meant to be generous and to share with those in need, but we selfishly hoard our resources for ourselves."[11] Reformed theology affirms that human beings are "sinful" and fall short of God's purpose and design for our lives. Paul states it well to the Romans: "I do not understand my own actions. For I do not do what I want, but I do the very thing that I hate."[12] Sin has been defined in many different ways, but perhaps an effective definition is "brokenness." As human beings, we are broken and we are guilty of turning to possessions to fill spiritual and psychological voids.

Purchasing and consuming goods gives us the illusion of power and completeness, but the illusion is always short lived. It is not long before we need something else. We rationalize our purchases by buying things "on sale," but that does not fix the problem because the problem is spiritual. Hamilton observes, "Too much of our energy and our thoughts and our heart's desire go into acquisition and pleasure, and there's nothing left to nurture the fruit God intends us to produce. Our spiritual lives remain immature and unfruitful as long as we're pursuing the American Dream dictated by our culture."[13] The fundamental problem with the American Dream is that it is built on the concept that enough is never enough. There is always more money to make, more people to impress, and more to buy. John Rockefeller was once asked, "How much is enough?" He responded by saying, "Just a little bit more." This is how many go through life: always pursuing just a little bit more. This indicates the spiritual void to which

Hamilton is referring. Augustine got it right centuries ago in his *Confessions* that "our heart is restless until we find our rest in God."[14] Materialism is only a temporary fix and still leaves a lingering spiritual void in our lives.

5) **Hauerwas reminds us that we are often possessed by our possessions, and discipleship involves constantly learning to become dispossessed.** Hauerwas states: "To become followers of Jesus means that we must, like him, be dispossessed of all that we think gives us power over our own lives and the lives of others. Unless we learn to relinquish our presumption that we can ensure the significance of our lives, we are not capable of the peace of God's kingdom."[15] Possessions provide a false sense of security, and, far too often, possessions end up owning us rather than the other way around. The rich young ruler went away sad simply because he was not willing to part with his possessions. His life was defined by what he had. We should enjoy our possessions but be able to stand apart from them.

Possessions also give us a false sense of control. The wealthiest people in our culture are often the most controlling. According to Hauerwas: "Since our 'control' and 'power' cannot help but be built on an insufficient basis, we must use force to maintain the illusion that we are in control. We are deeply afraid of losing what unity of self we have achieved. Any idea or person threatening that unity must either be manipulated or eliminated."[16] For Hauerwas, this desire for control then becomes a slippery slope to violence and manipulation. Possessions pose the greatest threat to authentic discipleship because there is great competition for our allegiance. But Jesus reminds us that "one's life does not consist in the abundance of possessions."[17] This is a far cry from what we hear from our culture.

6) **Hamilton and Hauerwas agree that fear is a universal and powerful force that often controls our approach to money and materialism.** We fear not having enough. We fear not being able to keep up with everybody else.

We fear what may or may not happen in the future. We fear feelings of inadequacy. Yet fear and anxiety are the opposite of faith. In the Epilogue to *Enough,* Hamilton provides three pieces of advice for learning to overcome fear.

i)   First, we are called to place authentic trust in God. This sounds obvious, but how many people actually live their lives truly trusting God with the future? "Trusting God is the first key to overcoming fear. We have the choice to see the giants in our lives and live in fear, to pretend that the giants are not there and bury our heads in the sand, or to say, 'Lord, I trust you. Bring something good from these difficult times. Guide my steps, and help me walk with you.'"[18] Excessive hoarding of money and possessions is often a key indication of someone who lives in a constant state of fear. Ironically, those with very little are more inclined to trust in God for the future. Why? They have fewer distractions and fewer allegiances.

ii) Second, he says that we should consistently offer gratitude. In a culture obsessed with acquiring more, we rarely stop to give thanks for what we already have. Gratitude can serve as an antidote to fear. Time spent being thankful is time we cannot spend being fearful.

iii) Third, and perhaps most importantly, Hamilton says that we can overcome fear by living lives of service and generosity to others. Materialism is usually the result of a selfish mentality in which we only focus on ourselves and our own needs. "Something happens when we take our eyes off ourselves and choose to serve others."[19] That shift from self to others is the heart of Christianity, but is very difficult in our culture.

Like Hamilton, Hauerwas also acknowledges that fear must be overcome and replaced with trust. "Trust is impossible in communities that always regard the other as a challenge and threat to their existence. One of the most profound commitments of a community, therefore, is providing a context that encourages us to trust and depend on one another."[20] This is a fundamental shift in mindset that must be modeled by the church. In an individualistic culture where many fear not having enough, we must trust in God and in each other that there will be enough. Christian community helps us to do this in multiple ways.

7) *Preachers are called to challenge all forms of politics and economics in light of the gospel.* It is often true that politics is viewed solely through the lens of self-interest. Although there are exceptions, those with higher incomes and higher net worths tend to vote Republican. Since the church is a place where diverse political ideologies coexist, preachers must remember that all political and economic views can and should be challenged in light of the gospel. In *Resident Aliens,* Hauerwas and Willimon say, "That which makes the church 'radical' and forever new is not that the church tends to lean toward the left on most social issues, but rather that the church knows Jesus whereas the world does not. In the church's view, the political left is not noticeably more interesting than the political right; both sides tend toward solutions that act as if the world has not ended and begun in Jesus. These 'solutions' are only mirror images of the status quo."[21] For Christians, Hauerwas and Willimon are arguing that politics should be viewed through the lens of the gospel. Christians are called to be faithful to God first, regardless of national and political ideologies. "We would like a church that again asserts that God, not nations, rules the world, that the boundaries of God's kingdom transcend those of Caesar, and that the main political task of the church is the formation of people who see clearly the cost of discipleship and are willing to pay the price."[22] It is impossible to follow Jesus if one is only concerned about economic or political self-interest. Self-centeredness stands in sharp contrast to Christian discipleship. As someone writing in Paul's name reminds Timothy, the

"love of money is a root of all kinds of evil"[23] and is often the reason that we forget we are citizens of God's Kingdom first. Jesus said, "If any want to become my followers, let them deny themselves and take up their cross and follow me."[24] The gospel cannot and should not be controlled, coerced, or manipulated by political ideology.

8) **Christian faith can and should serve as the conscience of capitalism.** The United States of America is a capitalistic culture. Although far from perfect, capitalism has lifted millions of people out of poverty and given opportunity to those who would otherwise not have it. It has also produced massive amounts of wealth that have been used for good in our nation and around the world. Ethicists such as John Howard Yoder have said that Christianity and capitalism are incompatible. This is a false dichotomy. In *Money, Greed, and God,* Jay Richards defends capitalism: "The twentieth century was one big lab experiment for the economic theories of the eighteenth and nineteenth centuries. The results of that experiment are in. It's time for Christians to take an honest look at the economic facts and get acquainted with capitalism."[25] Early in his life, Richards believed that true Christians would favor socialism if they really cared about the poor. After he gained a deeper understanding of economics, he changed his perspective. The collapse of the Soviet Union was pivotal for Richards.

Although capitalism drives free markets, Christianity should serve as its conscience. Specifically, Christians are called to abide by the law, pay taxes, be generous, and guard against greed. Those who succeed in the system have a moral obligation as followers of Christ to look out for those who are in need.

9) **Preachers must maintain and articulate high expectations when it comes to financial giving.** Many clergy hold low stewardship expectations

and should not be surprised when church members consistently meet those low expectations. The sixth hypothesis that Christian Smith and Michael Emerson state in their book *Passing the Plate* says: "American Christians do not give generously because their churches hold low expectations of financial giving— insecure church leadership and congregational cultures oriented toward avoiding possible offense soft-peddle expectations of faithful, generous giving."[26] Preachers and church leaders must be bold in the twenty-first century. "Previous studies suggest that the majority of U.S. clergy do not feel confident about maintaining high expectations in their congregations for financial contributions. Perhaps many clergy would rather have one percent of something rather than ten percent of nothing—if higher expectations were to turn parishioners off and away."[27] However, preachers should be clear that generous stewardship is not optional. Smith and Emerson show how Christian traditions that hold higher expectations of Christian giving are likely to have a much more generous membership than those who do not. Maintaining these expectations takes courage and audacity on the part of the preacher to be courageous and not shy away from the teachings of Christ. The gospels indicate that Jesus was clearly concerned about issues of stewardship and generosity, and his followers must be as well.

10) *Generosity is a liberating force that brings great joy into our lives.* Adam Hamilton states: "Our generosity to God and others not only touches God and other people, it also changes us. As human beings we were created with the need to be generous. When we are not generous in giving, we have a spiritual problem." He then continues: "We were created for generosity. Over time we become self-absorbed, money-consumed, joyless people. This is what a lifetime of financial and spiritual constipation looks like: joylessness."[28] Hauerwas agrees that we find joy when we stop turning to the material and superficial

to fill spiritual voids. "Perhaps the most remarkable aspect of learning to live joyfully is that we learn to see the simple and most common aspects of our existence, such as our friends, our spouses, our children, as sheer gifts to which we have no right but who are nonetheless present to us."[29] There is great wisdom in learning to live simply. Most of the time, the more we acquire, the more complicated our lives becomes.

Hauerwas is also clear that joy is not the same as happiness. "Happiness is too shallow a notion to characterize the disposition of the Christian, it too often suggests merely the satisfaction of desires determined by ourselves."[30] So many in our world think that happiness is life's ultimate goal. It is not. "Happiness, even in its most profound sense of satisfaction of a life well lived, lacks the sense of joy. The joy that characterizes the Christian life is not so much the fulfillment of any desire, but the discovery that we are capable of being people who not only desire peace but are peaceable. Joy thus comes to us as a gift that ironically provides us with the confidence in ourselves which makes possible our living of God's peace as a present reality."[31] Generosity liberates us because helping others leads to joy and joy leads to meaning and a sense of inner peace. We all long for inner peace. Materialism may make us temporarily happy, but, in the long run, it does not lead to sustaining joy and peace, only to a desire for more.

Some Closing Thoughts

You may or may not find these ten observations helpful. Some of them may resonate while others may not. What I do know is that as the church moves farther into the twenty-first century, our culture is becoming increasingly secular. Politics and social issues divide good people, and materialism is a growing problem. Christ offers timeless wisdom on these topics, but will we listen? Will we obey?

There is great speculation as to whether the church in North America will continue to decline and ultimately go the way of

Europe. Is there anything different about Christianity in this country? Dr. Frank Drowota, the founding pastor of Woodmont Christian Church (est. 1943), is believed to have said that he dreamed of a church that would "interpret truth in terms of the times, but challenge times in terms of the truth." Yet for many Christians today, there is clear disagreement as to when we should "interpret" and when we should "challenge." Many are now asking, "What is the church willing to stand for? Does it have the courage, conviction, and backbone to speak out to a constantly changing culture? What are the essentials?" These are certainly fair and relevant questions, but the answers are not easy to find. Even today, the authority, interpretation, and context of scripture are hotly debated among scholars and ministers, thereby significantly affecting how we answer these issues.

Swiss theologian Karl Barth is perhaps the greatest theologian of the twentieth century. Among other things, he became deeply concerned with the church's apathy and collaboration with Hitler's Nazi Germany, and for good reason. Today Barth is still speaking to us; he is still influential. His multi-volume work *Church Dogmatics* is still used with great benefit by both liberal and conservative scholars. According to Duke New Testament professor Richard Hays,

> Barth's prevailing concern was that if we conceive of ethics as the application of general principles to specific situations, we will in the end indulge our own wishes and whims, all the while claiming religious—or even biblical sanction. If so, we have poured the dictates and pronouncements of our own self-will into the empty container of a formal moral concept, thus giving them the aspect and dignity of an ethical claim (although, in fact, it is we ourselves who will them).[32]

When Jesus was asked which law is the greatest, we know how he responded: "Love the Lord your God with all your heart, soul, mind, and strength. And, love your neighbor as yourself." Yet we also acknowledge that Jesus gave specific instruction on issues that Christians continue to debate—adultery, divorce, marriage, taxes, retaliation, war, wealth, greed, possessions, and lust, to name just a few.

No doubt, the American Church and those of us who actively support it find ourselves in challenging times. But this is not the time for us to back down but for us to step up, perhaps in new ways and with a renewed message. French philosopher Alexis de Tocqueville visited this nation back in the nineteenth century to find out what made America great. He was surprised by what he found, and he offered these powerful insights:

> I sought for the greatness and genius of America in her commodious harbors and her ample rivers—and it was not there...in her fertile fields and boundless forests and it was not there...in her rich mines and her vast world commerce—and it was not there...in her democratic Congress and her matchless Constitution—and it was not there. Not until I went into the churches of America and heard her pulpits aflame with righteousness did I understand the secret of her genius and power. America is great because she is good, and if America ever ceases to be good, she will cease to be great.[33]

How will we as pastors and preachers help again move the church and even the nation toward that—and Who—that is good? Our answer to that question may turn out to be the most important and consequential of all.

Appendix

My Journey: From the Right to the Left and Back to the Center

✦ ✦ ✦ ✦ ✦ ✦ ✦ ✦ ✦ ✦ ✦ ✦ ✦ ✦

Sir Winston Churchill is attributed with saying, "If you're not a liberal at twenty, you have no heart, but if you're not a conservative at forty, you have no brain." My mother once quoted these words to me when I finished my Master of Divinity at Princeton Theological Seminary. Whenever a person writes about faith, politics, money, and materialism, many first want to know where that person is coming from. What is my agenda? What is my perspective? I can honestly say, as a thirty-five-year-old minister, I have been exposed to both ends of the spectrum and everything in between. At this point in my life, I would label myself as a raging moderate.

I was born and raised in Memphis, Tennessee, as the oldest of four children in an upper-middle-class household. My father is a third-generation Disciples of Christ minister (making me a fourth-generation one), trained at Vanderbilt Divinity School, and he too could be identified as a moderate, probably left of center. My mother is now deceased, but she was a former schoolteacher who became a homemaker and raised four children. She grew up in a more conservative family in Paris, Tennessee. Growing up, I can specifically remember presidential elections in which my mother and father would vote for different candidates. They did not always see eye to eye on political matters.

My father was and still is unafraid to bring politics into the pulpit, but he has always had a gift for finding the balance. I have heard from many church members over the years that they could never guess if he was a Republican or a Democrat. He has always told me he wants to be a Christian first. Yet he was heavily influenced by Walter Rauschenbusch and the Social Gospel movement as well as by the preaching of Harry Emerson

Fosdick, the founding pastor of The Riverside Church in New York City, a church that I would later serve in while in seminary.

Years ago my father taught me about Aristotle's "Golden Mean." Basically defined, it is "the desirable middle between two extremes." My father believes that following the Golden Mean is the best thing for preachers to do because we are called to minister to people of different politics and backgrounds. If you go too far one way or the other, it is possible to alienate and marginalize a large portion of your congregation, which would not be a good thing. This wisdom from my father has always stuck with me and served me well.

Growing up, I attended private schools in Memphis where most of my friends and their families were conservative Republicans. After graduating from high school, I decided to attend Texas Christian University in Fort Worth, Texas. It was a wonderful experience; I treasure those years. There I was surrounded by people who, with the exception of a few, were from conservative Republican families. This made sense given the geography and the affluence of those attending TCU. I spent my undergraduate years as a religion and sociology double major, but it was during college that my interest in politics began. I supported George W. Bush in the presidential election of 2000, a fascinating election that ended up in the Supreme Court of the United States. It was really Vice President Al Gore's election to lose, and somehow he managed to do just that. For many Americans, including myself, Bush's humor and down-to-earth rhetoric resonated and was much preferable to Al Gore's arrogance and elitist mentality. I can still remember Gore rolling his eyes to some of Bush's responses during the presidential debates. After weeks of controversy and ultimately a Supreme Court ruling, George Bush became the forty-third U.S. president and was inaugurated in January 2001. Nine months later, the world changed.

I was a senior in college and was in my fraternity house room when my phone rang on Tuesday morning, September 11, 2001. My mother was in town visiting, and it was her birthday. She was at her hotel and was calling to see if I was watching the news. I turned on the TV just in time to see the second plane hit the second tower at New York's World Trade Center, and then I watched, along with the rest of the country, as the Twin Towers fell. That day changed our world forever, although Stanley Hauerwas would respond by saying that the world changed in 33 c.e. My generation had never seen anything like that attack. Nineteen terrorists had collaborated together to hijack commercial airplanes and had turned them into missiles. Two planes hit the Twin Towers, one plane crashed into the side of the Pentagon, and a fourth plane, United Flight 93, was brought down by some very courageous souls on board who prevented it from hitting another famous target, most likely the Capitol or the White House. The attacks were the result of brainwashed Islamic fundamentalists who were willing to give their lives to destroy the lives of thousands of innocents. For those who ever doubted the connection between faith and politics, September 11 put to rest any doubt that the two are indeed intertwined.

Just nine months into his presidency, George W. Bush was charged with leading our nation through this horrific tragedy, and he did it well, at least in the short term. American unity and resolve were as high as they had ever been. Can't we all remember Bush standing on top of the rubble at Ground Zero with his arm around a weary firefighter, saying into a megaphone, "I can hear you, the world can hear you, and the people who knocked down these buildings will hear from all of us soon"? Three weeks later, I stood at Ground Zero with my father while on a trip up east to visit Princeton Seminary, Harvard, and Yale Divinity Schools. We ended the trip in New York City. Seeing the destruction in person really brought the reality of it home for me. September 11 had changed our world forever. The twenty-first century would be an age when faith and politics could not be separated, and the relationship between Christianity and Islam would never be the same.

I made the decision to attend Princeton Seminary in the fall of 2002. Although I had wrestled with deciding between seminary and law school, I felt God was calling me into the ministry. I loved Princeton. I loved the focus on local church ministry, the strong relationship with the Presbyterian Church (USA), and the balance that I found there between liberal and conservative voices theologically, politically, and socially (more so than Harvard, Yale, and Vanderbilt). At that time, I was a conservative Southern boy from Tennessee, who had been to college in Texas, and was now heading up to the "liberal" East Coast. I still supported George W. Bush. I felt he had done an excellent job of leading our country through September 11, had brought the nation together, and was working hard to bring those responsible to justice. Not everybody up East was as fond of the President as I was. This became clear very quickly. However, I was still able to maintain my position.

While in seminary, I also spent much of my time in New York City. A family friend owned an apartment there so I was able to come to New York often on the weekends and visit many of the churches there. My father had always told me about The Riverside Church and the impact that Harry Emerson Fosdick, William Sloane Coffin, and others had on his ministry, preaching, and education. I had heard Jim Forbes, the senior minister there, speak at Princeton, and I wanted to go and visit the church. I visited several times, and for some reason I became enamored with this incredibly "liberal" church on the upper west side of Manhattan. I really can't explain why. What I do know is that this began to mark a shift in my way of thinking. I loved Riverside's commitment to being international, interracial, and interdenominational. I loved the church's history and passion for mission and social justice.

In the spring of 2003, I had to line up a field education placement for the following year. I made an appointment with Rev. Paul Rauschenbusch, Riverside's minister for college and young adult ministry and the great-grandson of the famous Walter Rauschenbusch, founder of the Social Gospel movement. We hit it off. He offered me an internship for the following year. That summer, Rauschenbusch was hired by Princeton University to become the associate dean of religious life. Starting that fall of 2003, I basically inherited his job at Riverside as a part-time intern. Ultimately, I became the staff person working part-time with college students and young adults.

The Riverside years were formative and challenging for me. I was certainly out of my comfort zone, but I was also pushed and grew in many ways. I maintained a very busy schedule, spending half of my time in Princeton and half in New York. I enjoyed having one foot in the academy and the other foot in the church. Slowly, my politics began to change. Riverside is a church that speaks out against war—all war. Primarily, it was during the buildup to the war in Iraq that the Bush administration's attempt to link Saddam Hussein to September 11 seemed far-fetched to me. The combination of those two things brought me back to the middle with a deeper sensitivity to the left. Secretary of State Colin Powell's discomfort in making his case to the United Nations was a red flag. Something didn't seem right. Something was happening, and I knew that my worldview was gradually changing. Riverside played a big role in that.

There were many people I came into contact with during those years, but three had a profound impact on my shifting worldview—Dr. Jim Forbes, Dr. Jim Wallis, and Dr. Cornel West. Dr. Forbes was my boss at Riverside and is a mesmerizing preacher. His intellect and eloquence, along with his progressive principles and passion for the biblical text, were contagious. He was a mentor to me in many ways.

Then there was Jim Wallis. I was able to spend time with him at Princeton and Riverside. He is the chief editor of *Sojourners* magazine and a leading progressive voice in our nation on faith and politics. I have enjoyed reading his books and articles, and I admire the impact that he continues to have on public dialogue regarding faith and politics. He considers himself a "progressive evangelical." I like that phrase.

Cornel West left Harvard in 2002 for Princeton after a very public falling out with Harvard's president Lawrence Summers. Although I never had him for class at Princeton, I was able to spend time with him. He is a leading intellectual in areas of race, religion, and African American studies. I greatly admire the work that he has done in the areas of race, democracy, and, most recently, poverty.

All three of these men played an important role in the shifting of my worldview, and I am grateful to have spent time with each of them.

Jim Wallis's book *God's Politics: Why the Right Gets It Wrong and the Left Doesn't Get It* was published in 2005. Although many label him as a liberal, Wallis's book is a must read for anybody with an interest in faith, preaching, and politics. In the book, Wallis makes the claim that God is not a Republican or a Democrat. In the book's "Introduction," he says the following:

> God's politics reminds us of the people our politics always neglects—the poor, the vulnerable, the left behind. God's politics challenges narrow, national, ethnic, economic, or cultural self-interest, reminding us of a much wider world and the creative human diversity of all those made in the image of the creator. God's politics reminds us of the creation itself, a rich environment in which we are to be good stewards, not mere users, consumers, and exploiters. And God's politics pleads with us to resolve the inevitable conflicts among us, as much as is possible, without the terrible cost and the consequences of war. God's politics always reminds us of the ancient prophetic prescription to "choose life, so that you and your children may live," and challenges all the selective moralities that would choose one set of lives and issues over another.[1]

This book would go on to climb *The New York Times* bestseller list and has had a tremendous impact on many people, myself included. Wallis is certainly not as politically "balanced" as he claims to be, but his voice has been and continues to be important, especially when faith and politics intersect. He does an excellent job of looking at political issues through the lens of scripture and asking the difficult questions that need to be asked.

So, those were some of the basic reasons that my worldview and politics shifted during seminary.

I graduated from Princeton in May of 2005, and I decided to leave the East Coast and Riverside to return home to Memphis, Tennessee, to work with my father at my home church—Lindenwood Christian Church. While I was wrestling with the decision, Cornel West helped me by telling me there was much more work to be done in Memphis than in New York, but, primarily, I wanted to be closer to my family. I was ordained on May 22, 2005, in Memphis and started my ministry in June of that year. To put it mildly, many of my Southern friends wondered what had happened to me during the years up East. I had clearly changed and some did not understand why. Holding more progressive (a nicer word, for many, than liberal) positions in the South can be very challenging. I found myself in many heated debates and conversations. I learned a lot from those dialogues and exchanges.

Less than two years later, I was offered the opportunity to become the senior minister of Woodmont Christian Church in Nashville, Tennessee, at the young age of twenty-seven. I accepted the position but knew that I would be going to a more conservative congregation located in the heart of Green Hills in Nashville. In the Christian Church (Disciples of Christ), we claim to find unity within our diversity. This is true, but what you will often find is that geography can dictate to a large degree the politics and ethos of a congregation. Since coming to Woodmont, I have found myself moving more to the center right, which is where I feel most comfortable and transparent. I continue to wrestle with questions of war, poverty, gay marriage, health care, taxation, the role of government, greed, materialism, and what Christ calls us to do about these things. I have learned to embrace the dialogue as a gift and to challenge others to do the same. I am comfortable saying that I have now returned to the political center, not in an attempt to accommodate but because, in my heart, that is where I am most comfortable and most effective as a pastor and preacher. There are very good people on multiple sides of many issues. There are issues that call for us to take a definite stand, and I am not afraid to do so. But Aristotle's Golden Mean continues to be a worthy goal. I consider myself a moderate, and I am certainly at peace with that. I can preach and teach effectively to those on both the left and on the right, which is very important.

As I have reflected on the role church and politics have played over the last few decades, I have concluded that the Religious Right set the table for where we find ourselves today, but the mainline church has gone too far in the other direction. Now, those who are pro-life and pro-traditional marriage find themselves ostracized from the mainline church. They feel out of place. I moved towards the left during seminary but have moved back to the center right since. If the mainline church is to have any hope for the future, it must reopen its doors to moderates and reasonable conservatives or the continued demise is inevitable.

I also find myself still fascinated by the topic of money and materialism, not only because of Jesus' passionate teaching on the subject, but also because it is a universal reality that we are confronted with every day. Simply put, we live in a materialistic world. My context, Nashville's Green Hills, is becoming more and more commercialized. I believe that money, materialism, and a false sense of security in life pose the greatest challenge to the Christian faith in the United States. Those who have plenty often feel as though they do not need God. In fact, many believe they *are* God. Hauerwas is correct in saying that "idolatry" is the church's greatest challenge in the future. Of the many convictions I hold, perhaps none is greater than the belief that faithful preachers are called to consistently address the subjects of money, materialism, and idolatry from the pulpit and warn of the dangers of simply "storing up treasures on earth."

When I moved to Nashville in 2007, I met and fell in love with Megan Partridge of Waynesboro, Virginia. We were introduced through a mutual friend at a local fundraiser for the Boys and Girls Club of Middle Tennessee. We became engaged on Labor Day weekend of 2008 and were married at Woodmont Christian Church on May 16, 2009. Megan is an allergist in private practice with the Allergy, Asthma, and Sinus Center of Tennessee. She is beautiful on the inside and out. When she moved to Nashville, she prayed to meet a Christian husband. I told her to be careful what she prayed for. We are now blessed with two children: Montgomery Mae born July 7, 2010, and Clayton Robert born February 13, 2012. Being married to a physician has placed me in a higher socio-economic class, which is very different from what I experienced growing up as a preacher's kid. We are fortunate, and blessed in many ways. In recent years, this has caused me to wrestle even more with the issues that I have raised in this book. We live in a parsonage next to the church, although we certainly do not have to. I often find myself asking many questions: How should we live? What type of cars should we drive? How much should we give away? Where should our kids go to school? Wrestling with money and materialism in my own life continues to be a personal and professional struggle.

In my ministry context in Nashville's Green Hills, one of the most commercialized parts of our city, I am certainly not alone in this struggle. I am absolutely fascinated with what money does to people—both good and bad. Somebody once said, "Money makes a great servant but a terrible master." I am also fascinated by how quickly many Christians completely dismiss and ignore Jesus' teachings about money and possessions. Politics and money are issues that preachers must address from the pulpit, despite the discomfort. Money, materialism, and consumerism are false gods in our culture. All human beings who follow Christ, if they are honest, should wrestle with the tension. How much is too much? At what point do we become materialistic? How can we guard against greed? Why are we never satisfied? Generosity is a liberating force, although many fail to experience it. Jesus has set forth a challenge that we will all wrestle with for the rest of our lives.

Notes

Chapter 1: Preachers, Politics, and Partisanship

[1]Christian Church (Disciples of Christ) website, accessed January 12, 2015, http://www.disciples.org.

[2]Jon Meacham, *American Gospel: God, the Founding Fathers, and the Making of a Nation* (New York: Random House, 2006), 5.

[3]*Declaration of Independence,* 1776, accessed October 10, 2014, http://www.archives.gov/exhibits/charters/declaration_transcript.html.

[4]Walter Brueggemann, *Disruptive Grace: Reflections on God, Scripture, and the Church,* ed. Carolyn Sharp (Minneapolis: Fortress Press, 2011), 314.

[5]Mike Slaughter, Charles Gutenson, and Robert Jones, *Hijacked: Responding to the Partisan Church Divide* (Nashville: Abingdon Press, 2012), 42.

[6]Ibid., 43–44.

[7]Ibid., 44.

[8]Jonathan Haidt, *The Happiness Hypothesis* (New York: Basic Books, 2006), 242.

[9]Slaughter, Gutenson, and Jones, *Hijacked*, 49–50.

[10]Ibid., 50.

[11]Ibid., 108.

[12]Ibid.

[13]Robert D. Putnam and David E. Campbell, *American Grace: How Religion Divides and Unites Us* (New York: Simon and Schuster, 2010), 428.

[14]Ibid., 375.

[15]Ibid., 434.

[16]Jim Wallis, *Rediscovering Values on Wall Street, Main Street, and Your Street* (New York: Simon and Schuster, 2010), 50.

[17]Ibid., 57.

[18]Ibid., 116–17.

[19]Ibid., 121–22.

[20]Philippians 4:11b–12a.

[21]Haidt, *The Happiness Hypothesis*, 99.

[22]Paul Froese and Christopher Bader, *America's Four Gods: What We Say About God and What That Says About Us* (New York: Oxford Press, 2010), 24.

[23]Ibid., 122.

[24]Ibid., 124.

[25]Christian Smith, Michael Emerson, and Patricia Snell, *Passing the Plate: Why American Christians Don't Give Away More Money (*New York: Oxford Press, 2008), 58–59.

Chapter 2: Jesus' Political and Economic Agenda

[1]Luke 4:17–19, 21b.

[2]John Howard Yoder, *The Politics of Jesus* (Cambridge, England: Eerdmans, 2d ed., 1994), 32.

[3]Ibid., 32.

[4]Ibid., 49.

[5]Harvey Cox, *When Jesus Came to Harvard* (New York: Mariner Books, 2004), 226.

[6]Yoder, *The Politics of Jesus,* 52–53.

[7]Luke 6:20–26.

[8]William Barclay, *The Daily Study Bible Series: The Gospel of Luke* (Louisville: Westminster John Knox Press, rev. ed., 1975), 76.

[9]Luke 6:27–36.

[10]Barclay, *The Gospel of Luke,* 78.

[11]William Brosend, *Conversations with Scripture: The Parables* (Harrisburg, Pa.: Morehouse Publishing, 2006), 11.

[12]Luke 10:27.

[13]Brosend, *Conversations with Scripture,* 96.

[14]Ibid., 97.

[15]Ibid., 78.

[16]Richard Lischer, *Reading the Parables,* Interpretation Series (Louisville: Westminster John Knox Press, 2014), 35–36.

[17]Brosend, *Conversations with Scripture,* 79–80.

[18]Luke 12:15b.

[19]Barclay, *The Gospel of Luke,* 193.

[20]Ibid., 194.

[21]Brosend, *Conversations with Scripture,* 87.

[22]Ibid.

[23]Luke 19:45–48.

[24]Barclay, *The Gospel of Luke,* 242.

[25]Luke 20:21–22.

[26]Luke 20:24–25.

[27]Barclay, *The Gospel of Luke,* 248–49.

[28]The gospel accounts also make it clear that Jesus was a threat to some in the religious establishment (Mark 3:6; 14:1; John 11:45–57; 12:9–11).

[29]Yoder, *The Politics of Jesus,* 129.

[30]Ibid.

[31]Marcus J. Borg and John Dominic Crossan, *The Last Week: What the Gospels Really Teach About Jesus' Last Days in Jerusalem* (New York: Harper Collins, 2006), 161.

[32]Ibid., 162.

[33]Amy-Jill Levine, "Jesus and the Voting Booth," unpublished speech to Nashville's Downtown Rotary Club (July 16, 2012). Used by permission.

[34]Matthew 25:14–30.

[35]Brosend, *Conversations with Scripture,* 67.

[36]Lischer, *Reading the Parables,* 91.

[37]Ibid.

[38]Matthew 25:40.

Chapter 3: Stanley Hauerwas on Greed, Desire, and Possessions

[1]Luke 12:15.

[2]Stanley Hauerwas, "Can Greed Be a Good?" in *Religion and Ethics* (June 9, 2010), accessed December 8, 2014, http://www.abc.net.au/religion/articles/2010/06/09/2922773.htm.

[3]Ibid.

[4]Ibid.

[5]Stanley Hauerwas and Will Willimon, *The Truth About God: The Ten Commandments in Christian Life* (Nashville: Abingdon Press, 1999), 132.

[6]Ibid.

[7]Ibid., 133.

[8]Ibid., 130.

[9]Ibid., 134.

[10]Ibid.

[11]Arthur C. Brooks, "The Downside of Inciting Envy," *The New York Times* (March 1, 2014), accessed March 24, 2014, http://www.nytimes.com/2014/03/02/opinion/sunday/the-downside-of-inciting-envy.html?_r=0.

[12]Ibid.

[13]Ibid.

[14]Hauerwas and Willimon, *The Truth About God*, 134–135.

[15]Ibid.,

[16]Ibid.

[17]Ibid.

[18]Stanley Hauerwas, *The Peaceable Kingdom* (Notre Dame, Ind.: University of Notre Dame Press, 1983), 86.

[19]Ibid.

[20]Ibid., 86–87.

[21]Matthew 7:3–5.

[22]Hauerwas, *The Peaceable Kingdom*, 87.

[23]Ibid., 148.

[24]Ibid.

[25]Ibid., 47.

[26]Ibid.

[27]Stanley Hauerwas and William H. Willimon, *Resident Aliens: Life in the Christian Colony* (Nashville: Abingdon Press, 1989), 131.

[28]Ibid.

[29]Hauerwas and Willimon, *The Truth About God*, 34.

[30]Ibid., 36.

[31]Charles Taylor, *A Secular Age* (Cambridge, Mass.: Harvard Press, 2007).

[32]Stanley Hauerwas, *Hannah's Child: A Theologian's Memoir* (Grand Rapids, Mich.: Eerdmans, 2010), x.

[33]Hauerwas and Willimon, *The Truth About God*, 36.

[34]Ibid.

[35]Matthew 6:24d.

[36]Hauerwas and Willimon, *The Truth About God*, 138.

[37]Stephen H. Webb, "The Very American Stanley Hauerwas," *First Things* (June 2002), accessed November 14, 2014, http://www.firstthings.com/article/2002/06/the-very-american-stanley-hauerwas.

[38]Duke University website, accessed February 10, 2014, http://admissions.duke.edu/education/value.

[39]Hauerwas and Willimon, *The Truth About God,* 130.

[40]Webb, "The Very American Stanley Hauerwas."

[41]Jay Richards, *Money, Greed, and God* (New York: Harper One, 2009), 31.

[42]Hauerwas and Willimon, *The Truth About God,* 134.

[43]Richards, *Money, Greed, and God*, 124.

Chapter 4: Adam Hamilton's Passion for the "Radical Center"

[1]Adam Hamilton, *Seeing Gray in a World of Black and White* (Nashville: Abingdon Press, 2008), 5–6.

[2]Ibid., 8.

[3]Ibid.

[4]Ibid., 233.

[5]Adam Hamilton, *Confronting the Controversies: Biblical Perspectives on Tough Issues* (Nashville: Abingdon Press, 2005), 11.

[6]Hamilton, *Seeing Gray in a World of Black and White*, 235.

[7]Adam Hamilton, *Enough: Discovering Joy Through Simplicity and Generosity* (Nashville: Abingdon Press, 2009), 14–15, quoting Alexis de Tocqueville, *Democracy in America* (London: Penguin, 2003), 534, 713.

[8]Hamilton, *Enough*, 15.

[9]Ibid., 16.

[10]Ibid., 17.

[11]Ibid., 18.

[12]Ibid., 24–25.

[13]Ibid., 31.

[14]John 10:10b.

[15]Hamilton, *Enough*, 71.

[16]Ibid., 71–72.

[17]Philippians 4:11b–12.

[18]Hamilton, *Enough*, 78.

[19]Philippians 4:8.

[20]Hamilton, *Enough*, 78.

[21]1 Thessalonians 5:18a.

[22]Hamilton, *Enough*, 80.

[23]Armand Nicholi Jr., "Hope in a Secular Age," in *Finding God at Harvard: Spiritual Journeys of Thinking Christians,* edited by Kelly Monroe (Grand Rapids, Mich.: Zondervan, 1996), 114.

[24]Hamilton, *Enough*, 82.

[25]Ibid., 82–83.

[26]Ibid., 144.

[27]Ibid., 145.

[28]Ibid., 104-105.

[29]Ibid., 118.

[30]Ibid., 119.

[31]Hauerwas, *The Peaceable Kingdom* (Notre Dame, Ind.: University of Notre Dame Press, 1983), 148.

[32]Hamilton, *Enough*, 103.

[33]Ibid., 110.

[34]Adam Hamilton, "Lessons from Moses," 2013 Inaugural Prayer Service Sermon, Washington National Cathedral, January 22, 2013.

[35]Ibid.

[36]Ibid.

[37]Ibid.

Chapter 5: Preaching in a Materialistic Culture

[1]Eugene H. Peterson, *The Pastor* (New York: Harper Collins, 2011), 5–6.

[2]Ibid.,6.

[3]Adam Hamilton, *Confronting the Controversies: Biblical Perspectives on Tough Issues* (Nashville: Abingdon Press, 2005), 11.

[4]Matthew 6:21.

[5]Friedrich Nietzsche, *The Dawn of Day,* trans. J. M. Kennedy (London: Allen and Unwin, 1911), 209–10.

[6]Timothy Keller, *Counterfeit Gods* (New York: Dutton Press, 2009), 58.

[7]Andrew Carnegie, as quoted in Joseph Frazier Wall, *Andrew Carnegie* (Pittsburgh, Pa.: Pittsburgh Press, 1989), 224–25.

[8]Matthew 6:19–21, 24.

[9]Stanley Hauerwas and Will Willimon, *The Truth About God: The Ten Commandments in Christian Life* (Nashville: Abingdon Press, 1999), 134.

[10]Ibid.

[11]Adam Hamilton, *Enough: Discovering Joy Through Simplicity and Generosity* (Nashville: Abingdon Press, 2009), 24–25.

[12]Romans 7:15.

[13]Hamilton, *Enough*, 28.

[14]Augustine, quoted in Peter Brown, *Augustine of Hippo: A Biography* (Berkeley, Calif.: University of California Press, 1969).

[15]Stanley Hauerwas, *The Peaceable Kingdom* (Notre Dame, Ind.: University of Notre Dame Press, 1983), 86.

[16]Ibid., 47.

[17]Luke 12:15b.

[18]Hamilton, *Enough,* 148.

[19]Ibid., 152.

[20]Stanley Hauerwas, as quoted in John Berkmann and Michael Cartwright, eds., *The Hauerwas Reader* (Durham, N.C.: Duke University Press, 2001), 135.

[21]Stanley Hauerwas and William H. Willimon, *Resident Aliens*: *Life in the Christian Colony* (Nashville: Abingdon Press, 1989), 28.

[22]Ibid., 48.

[23]1 Timothy 6:10a.

[24]Mark 8:34.

[25]Jay Richards, *Money, Greed, and God* (New York: Harper One, 2009), 5.

[26]Christian Smith, Michael Emerson, and Patricia Snell, *Passing the Plate: Why American Christians Don't Give Away More Money (*New York: Oxford Press, 2008), 82.

[27]Ibid., 83.

[28]Hamilton, *Enough,* 118.

[29]Hauerwas, *The Peaceable Kingdom*, 148.

[30]Ibid., 147.

[31]Ibid.

[32]Richard B. Hays, *The Moral Vision of the New Testament* (New York: Harper Collins, 1996), 228.

[33]Alexis de Tocqueville, *Democracy in America,* trans. Harvey Mansfield and Delba Winthrop (Chicago: University of Chicago Press, 2000).

Appendix

[1]Jim Wallis, *God's Politics: Why the Right Gets It Wrong and the Left Doesn't Get It* (New York: Harper Collins, 2005), xv.

Bibliography

Barclay, William. *The Daily Study Bible Series: The Gospel of Luke.* Louisville: Westminster John Knox, revised ed., 1975.

Berkmann, John, and Michael Cartwright, eds. *The Hauerwas Reader.* Durham, N.C.: Duke University Press, 2001.

Borg, Marcus J., and John Dominic Crossan. *The Last Week: What the Gospels Really Teach About Jesus' Last Days in Jerusalem.* New York: Harper Collins, 2006.

Brosend, William. *Conversations with Scripture: The Parables.* Harrisburg, Pa.: Morehouse Publishing, 2006.

Brooks, Arthur C. "The Downside of Inciting Envy," *The New York Times,* March 1, 2014. Accessed March 24, 2014. http://www.nytimes.com/2014/03/02/opinion/sunday/the-downside-of-inciting-envy.html?_r=0.

Brown, Peter. *Augustine of Hippo: A Biography.* Berkeley, Calif.: University of California Press, 1969.

Brueggemann, Walter. *Disruptive Grace: Reflections on God, Scripture, and the Church,* edited by Carolyn Sharp. Minneapolis: Fortress Press, 2011.

Cox, Harvey. *When Jesus Came to Harvard.* New York: Mariner Books, 2004.

Froese, Paul, and Christopher Bader. *America's Four Gods: What We Say About God and What That Says About Us.* New York: Oxford Press, 2010.

Haidt, Jonathan. *The Happiness Hypothesis.* New York: Basic Books, 2006.

Hamilton, Adam. *Seeing Grey in a World of Black and White.*

———. *Confronting the Controversies: Biblical Perspectives on Tough Issues.* Nashville: Abingdon Press, 2005.

———. *Enough: Discovering Joy Through Simplicity and Generosity.* Nashville: Abingdon Press, 2009.

———. "Lessons from Moses." 2013 Inaugural Prayer Service Sermon. Washington National Cathedral, January 22, 2013.

Hauerwas, Stanley. "Can Greed Be a Good?" *Religion and Ethics,*

June 9, 2010. Accessed December 8, 2014. http://www. abc.net.au/religion/articles/2010/06/09/2922773.htm.

———. *The Peaceable Kingdom.* Notre Dame, Ind.: University of Notre Dame Press, 1983

———. *Hannah's Child: A Theologian's Memoir.* Grand Rapids, Mich.: Eerdmans, 2010.

Hauerwas, Stanley, and Will Willimon. *The Truth About God: The Ten Commandments in Christian Life.* Nashville: Abingdon Press, 1999.

———. *Resident Aliens: Life in the Christian Colony.* Nashville: Abingdon Press, 1989.

Keller, Timothy. *Counterfeit Gods.* New York: Dutton Press, 2006.

Levine, Amy-Jill. "Jesus and the Voting Booth." Speech to Nashville's Downtown Rotary Club, July 16, 2012.

Lischer, Richard. *Reading the Parables (Interpretation Series),* Louisville: Westminster John Knox, 2014.

Meacham, Jon. *American Gospel: God, the Founding Fathers and the Making of a Nation.* New York: Random House, 2006.

Monroe, Kelly Ed. *Finding God at Harvard: Spiritual Journeys of Thinking Christians.* Grand Rapids, Mich.: Zondervan, 1996.

Nietzsche, Friedrich. *The Dawn of Day,* trans. J.M. Kennedy. London: Allen and Unwin, 1911.

Peterson, Eugene H. *The Pastor.* New York: Harper Collins, 2011.

Putnam, Robert D., and David E. Campbell. *American Grace: How Religion Divides and Unites Us.* New York: Simon and Schuster, 2010.

Richards, Jay. *Money, Greed, and God.* New York: Harper One, 2009.

Slaughter, Mike, Charles Gutenson, and Robert Jones. *Hijacked: Responding to the Partisan Church Divide.* Nashville: Abingdon Press, 2012.

Smith, Christian, Michael Emerson, and Patricia Snell. *Passing the Plate: Why American Christians Don't Give Away More Money.* New York: Oxford Press, 2008.

Taylor, Charles. *A Secular Age.* Cambridge, Mass.: Harvard Press, 2007.

The Holy Bible (New Revised Standard Version). Grand Rapids,

Mich.: Zondervan, 1989.

Wall, Joseph Frazier. *Andrew Carnegie*. Pittsburgh, Pa.: Pittsburgh Press, 1989.

Wallis, Jim. *Rediscovering Values on Wall Street, Main Street, and Your Street.*
New York: Simon and Schuster, 2010.

———. *God's Politics: Why the Right Gets It Wrong and the Left Doesn't Get It.*
New York: Harper Collins, 2005.

Webb, Stephen H. "The Very American Stanley Hauerwas," *First Things,* June 2002. Accessed November 14, 2014. http://www.firstthings.com/article/2002/06/the-very-american-stanley-hauerwas.

Yoder, John Howard. *The Politics of Jesus*. Cambridge, Mass.: Eerdmans, 2nd edition, 1994.